Life With WINE

A Practical Guide To The Basics

Dick Patton

LIFE WITH WINE
A Practical Guide to the Basics

Library of Congress Catalog Card Number: 94-92254

ISBN 0-9642885-0-8   9.95

Published by
Richard J. Patton, Communication, San Diego, CA

Design and typeset by
KIM ART, Grass Valley, CA

Printed by
Griffin Printing & Lithograph Co. Inc., Glendale, CA

Edited by Susan Wolbarst
Cover Watercolor by Jerianne Van Dijk

To Bern Ramey, who started it all.
To Charlotte, who stayed with me all the way.
And to Scott, Kim and Lisa, who share the fun.

Also, my thanks to Leon Santoro, friend and winemaker,
whose constant nudging and enthusiastic encouragement
keeps the motor running. And for his professional
review of the manuscript.

Dick Patton
San Diego, 1994

Welcome to the wonderful world of wine!

Dick Patton

12/94

Contents

Contents

Justification

Having said the world does not need another wine book, I hasten to explain—why this? There are hundreds of good books about wine and several reference encyclopedias that are essential in the pursuit of wine knowledge. Yet, several years ago as I prepared to teach a beginning course in wine, I could not find what I considered to be a suitable textbook. Those available did not provide concise, basic instruction in what I deemed a logical sequence. The information was good and attractively presented, but required one to leaf to and fro in order to round up and consolidate the desired information.

I have different views on what should come first and what should be included in beginning wine instruction. So, I solved the problem by writing my own course, which has been successful, and from whence this booklet springs.

If I have succeeded in simplifying a complicated subject by presenting the basics clearly and in an orderly manner, then you will know more about wine, what you need to know, with a minimum of effort and confusion.

Don't be critical if you sense something has been left out. I have worked diligently to make sure that much has been left out...and only the right things included. My hope is that this booklet will fill a niche in a sea of wine writing. And that it will leave you thirsting for more wine knowledge. If so, go for it. A list of some of the biggies in wine is near the back. I have referred to them liberally. And so should you.

"For they wished to fill the winepress of eloquence not with the tendrils of mere words but with the rich grape juice of good sense."
ST. JEROME

Appreciation

I think wine makes life better. With my interest, plus all of wine's attributes, it certainly makes life better for me. If you don't drink wine regularly, you may not share my enthusiasm. I'd like to change that, but I probably can't and maybe I shouldn't. What I can do is share some of my perceptions about wine and the effect it has on people who imbibe it moderately and with discernment.

Wine is a natural food. As such, it just naturally goes with and enhances the food we eat. I could no more sit down to a nice stew without a glass of red wine than you could go without your morning coffee. Wine turns an ordinary meal or get-together into an occasion. None can remain aloof where wine is served—it relaxes and warms a gathering, it brings us together at our best and it stimulates conversation and the flow of ideas. At home, across the United States or in a foreign land, wine is the universal ingredient that breaks barriers, furthers under-standing and promotes good fellowship. With a little knowledge of wine, which I am about to impart, and appreciation, which you must provide, you will become at home and at ease almost anywhere in the world.

Perhaps best of all, wine, this marvelous creation of nature, is ours to enjoy as we choose, without social dictates or eco-nomic restraints. Its variety is infinite. It is the moderate mood enhancer, available for all tastes and purses. And now we learn wine can be beneficial to our health. But of course.

Wine just makes life better and the more you know about it, the more you'll enjoy and appreciate it—all the days of your life.

"Water separates the people of the world, wine unites them."
ANONYMOUS

The Beginnings

About 8000 years ago—now don't get edgy, a little wine history is necessary, to sort of settle you in. It goes like this...

6000 B.C.   Evidence of vine cultivation and winemaking.

3000 B.C.   Records of grape growing and winemaking in Persia, Egypt and elsewhere. Hieroglyphics and drawings. Hundreds of references in the Bible.

500 B.C.   Romans led in developing grape-growing and winemaking throughout Europe. Each move of civilization spread wine through Italy, Spain, France and Germany.

A.D. 1500   From the fall of Rome in A.D. 476 and for 1000 years the Church controlled winemaking.

A.D. 1770   Franciscan Father Junipero Serra made first wine in California from the Mission grape at Mission San Diego de Alcala.

A.D. 1840   Mission life fading. Serious plantings begun around Los Angeles. '49 gold rush accelerated industry. Count Agoston Haraszthy, called Father of California viticulture, settled in San Diego.

A.D. 1855   Official Classification of Bordeaux red wines of the Medoc. Beginnings of organizing and controlling the wine trade in France and a model for the world.

A.D. 1870-90   Phylloxera (plant louse) devastated California and European vineyards. Replanted on native-American (eastern) vine stocks which were resistant.

1920-33   U.S. Prohibition (Volsted Act). 14 years of turmoil and billions of dollars wasted. Wine industry almost destroyed.

1946   After World War II the U.S. wine revolution began. New techniques and varietal plantings were promoted by such visionaries as Amerine, Lichine and Schoonmaker.

1994   U.S. one of largest wine producers and among the best in quality in the world.

There, we covered 8000 years of wine history in about a minute. And now you see that wine has not just suddenly become fashionable as a substitute for the dry martini. Since the beginning of civilization it has been cultivated, it has been an integral part of religious ceremonies and it has been ever present as man evolved into a discriminating social being. What we have today is the refinement of centuries of grape growing and winemaking. It just keeps getting better.

"Quickly, bring me a beaker of wine, so that I may wet my mind and say something clever."

ARISTOPHANES

Types of Grapes

We're Concerned With Only One

There are about 40 species (types) of grapes and thousands of varieties. Fortunately only two species are meaningful in the United States and only one of them is important to us.

Vitis Vinifera

Vitis Vinifera is the species that's grown in California and Europe and provides for over 90% of the wines of the world including such classic white varieties as Chardonnay and Sauvignon Blanc and reds like Cabernet Sauvignon and Pinot Noir. We are concerned only with these Vitis Vinifera, or European, varietals. They are the grapes that make the wines we know and love in California, France, Italy, Spain, Germany, Australia and around the world.

Vitis Labrusca

Vitis Labrusca is a native North American species grown in the New York Finger Lakes region, some midwestern states and parts of Canada. You know some of the varieties as Concord, Catawba and Niagara. But you won't find 'em in California. References to these grapes appear primarily in the chapter on Wines of Other States.

Types of Wine

Four Will Cover It

As a broad classification there are four types of wine: Table, Aperitif, Dessert, and Sparkling.

Table Wines

Table wines are just what the name implies. White, red or rosé still wines to go with food or to enjoy alone. Relatively low in alcohol, between 7% and 14%.

White Wines are made from white (sometimes called green) grapes. Pale straw to gold color.

Red Wines are made from red (sometimes called black) grapes. Fermented on their skins to pick up desired flavor and color.

Rosé or Blush Wines are made from red grapes. The juice of most grapes is white, they pick up their pretty pink shades from brief time on the skins during fermentation.

Aperitif Wines

Aperitif (appetizer) wines such as Vermouth, Dubonnet, Campari and Pernod are usually drunk before a meal to stimulate the appetite. Using a base wine, flavoring and herbs are added to create their own unique tastes. High alcohol content.

Dessert or Fortified Wines

Port, Madeira, and Sherry are examples. At a certain point during fermentation the base wine is fortified—brandy is added, which stops fermentation and leaves some natural sugar. The result is a distinctive sweet wine with high (17% to 21%) alcohol.

Sparkling Wines

You think of Champagne, right? Because the word is in general use to describe almost any sparkling wine. The French hate that, since their laws decree that only sparkling wine from the Champagne district may be so labeled. (Remember when we called our blue cheese Roquefort? They won that one.) Sparkling wines are made in many countries using various methods and grapes. They can be white, pink or red with alcohol levels about the same as in still table wines.

How Wine Is Made

The Four Types Have Their Differences

First you take some grapes and mush them all up. Then you ferment the juice and bottle it. And you'll have wine, of a sort. My mother-in-law, with a reputation as a great cook, responded to requests for her recipes in much the same manner. Her recipes were not written out, she just knew what was needed—a pinch of this, a dollop of that and then cook until done. No one could reproduce her dishes from those sketchy instructions; that's how she stayed famous. Making good wine is a more complicated task and mother nature is given a great deal of assistance these days. You'll appreciate more what you drink if you know more about what it takes to get it into the bottle.

The process of fermentation is what turns grape juice into wine. As grapes mature they develop a dusty coating on the skins. These are the yeast organisms that start fermentation that converts the natural grape sugar into alcohol. Today, this is not left to chance; cultured yeasts are introduced by the winemaker. If the grapes survive late rain, hail, frost, blight and other disasters, the grape bunches are cut from the vines at just the right moment of ripeness and brought to the winery, where they are dumped into a crusher-destemmer (which does just that) and then to a press that gently squeezes out the remaining juice.

Table Wines

For white wine, white grapes are crushed and pressed, then cool fermented for a week or two in stainless steel tanks. For dry wine, the yeasts are allowed to convert all sugar to alcohol.

If sweetness is desired, fermentation is stopped at the desired sugar level. After fermentation, the wine is racked (drained) off, leaving settled particles behind, then filtered and bottled. Unless the winemaker decides some aging in tanks or oak barrels will improve flavor.

For red wine, red grapes are crushed and destemmed. The juice, including skins and seeds (the "must"), is then transferred to fermentation tanks. During fermentation the juice is pumped over the skins to extract color and to develop flavor and body. After fermentation, the skins are gently pressed to extract the remaining wine. The wine is then transferred to large wooden or stainless steel tanks for aging, and later into small oak barrels for additional aging. During aging, which may be for a few months to several years, the wine mellows, develops bouquet and depth of flavor. The wine is then filtered and bottled (some don't filter, more natural, you know). It may be further aged in the bottle before release.

For rosé or blush wines the process is similar to making white wines except that red grapes are used and the juice left on the skins just long enough to extract the desired color and flavor.

Aperitif and Dessert Wines

In the section on Types of Wines, I briefly described what makes aperitif (flavored) and dessert (fortified) wines what they are. It's probably all you want or need to know, so let's move along.

Sparkling Wines

Sparkling wines start out being still wine. Several lots of these wines are blended to achieve the balance and flavors desired by the winemaker. The wine then undergoes a second fermentation which produces the bubbles. There are three methods used to make sparkling wine.

Methode Champenoise—The traditional method used to make real French Champagne and many other sparkling wines. A mixture of yeast and sugar is added to the wine and it is bottled. A temporary cap is applied, the wine is stored and the second fermentation takes place, producing the bubbles. Bottles are then placed in racks neck down and are shaken and turned to force sediment into the neck of the bottle. After several weeks the neck is frozen, the cap removed and the sediment plug expelled. The space left is filled and the bottle receives its final cork. It is then cellared for aging, from 12 to 18 months or more. That explains why wine made by this method is more expensive. The wine has never left the bottle it started in. The label may read, Fermented In *This* Bottle.

Transfer Method—A mixture of yeast and sugar is added to the base wine. It is then bottled for a second fermentation. After fermentation, bottles are emptied into tanks, the wine is filtered, then transferred to another bottle. The process is complete in a few months. Produces some good sparkling wines at a moderate price. The label may read, Fermented In *The* Bottle.

Charmat or Bulk Method—The base wine is moved to tanks where the yeast-sugar mixture is added and the second fermentation takes place. The wine is then filtered and bottled. Just a few weeks to make these inexpensive bubblies.

The Grapes Used—In California there are no restrictions, as there are in France, as to what grapes can be used to make sparkling wine. Chardonnay and Pinot Noir are the traditional grapes used, but there is also some blending of Chenin Blanc and Pinot Blanc. Most California sparkling wines, whether made from white or red grapes, are white or slightly pink.

Interpreting Dryness or Sweetness—Some of the terms used on wine labels can be misleading.

Natural or Ultra Brut—bone dry, no sugar.

Brut—dry, about .05% to 1.0% sugar.

Extra Dry—slightly sweet, 1.0% to 2.0% sugar.

Demi-Sec—Means half-dry, but it's sweet, up to 5.0% sugar.

THE WINES OF
California

Why We Start Here

Let's jump right in and start with the wines of California. Not because we are C.C.'s (California Chauvinists), but because it just makes sense to start here. Think of California as a wine country onto itself. It has a multitude of viticultural areas uniquely suited to grape growing and the production of some of the best wines in the world. Wines that are readily available in shops and stores that carry what they decide, at prices influenced by competition, not government mandate. There is a well made wine for every taste in every price range, and lots of it.

I mentioned earlier that most books on wine don't put things in the right order, for us. Presumptuous perhaps, but heck, probably all of you reading this live somewhere in the United States. Then why start with France, as most wine books do, when California produces almost 90% of the wine made in the United States and about 70% of the wine that's consumed in the United States?

I suppose those books start with French wines because they are written for a larger audience, and because France produces one-fifth of all the world's wine and the finest wines in the world. France just sets the standards by which all wines are judged. But French wines are also much more difficult to sort out. They are named after districts, communes, chateaux, provinces, villages, vineyards and sometimes the grape itself.

Whereas California, with some exceptions, keeps it simple by using the varietal name of the grape on the label.

Most of the grape varieties used in California wines are the same varieties that are used to make French wines.

So, you'll find it easier to learn about California wines if we start with them and learn about the grapes that are used and the wines they make. It will then be easier to learn about French wines because you'll already know about the grapes that are used. *N'est ce pas?*

Varietal, Generic and Proprietary Wines Explained

Varietal Wines

Wines that take their names from the grapes used are called varietal wines. Mostly we do that in California. We make identification easier than the French by labeling our wines after such classic white grapes as Chardonnay and Sauvignon Blanc and the fine red grapes such as Cabernet Sauvignon and Merlot. These are varieties of grapes—when you see one of these names on a label you are assured by law that at least 75% of the wine consists of that grape. You may not care for what you're drinking, but at least you'll know what you're drinking.

Generic Wines

California wines labeled Chablis and Burgundy are in this generic category. They're not varietals—no grape name. They are usually inexpensive jug wines made from a blend of various grapes. Actually, Chablis and Burgundy are legally defined areas in

France with strict regulations as to the grapes used. You're familiar with other generics labeled as Sauterne, Rhine Wine and Sherry—which are legally defined areas in France, Germany and Spain. California generics usually bear little resemblance to their namesakes but they are often very good wines in their category. It becomes a matter of your generic taste preference— as it should.

As proof that most everything has its exceptions, several California wineries are now producing what are called, *Fighting Varietals*. These are inexpensive varietal wines, labeled for the grape used, and often put up in liter-and-a-half bottles. It may not be right to hang the tag, "jug wine" on them, they are usually quite pleasant, represent good value and are a step up from the generic jugs.

Proprietary Wines

These are wines with names given to them by the producer, who hopes that the goodness of the product will create its own recognition and acceptance. Which is just what happened to such proprietary wines as Blue Nun, Lancers, Partage' and Mouton Cadet. Then closer to home, Marlstone, Opus One, Refrigerator White, Le Cigare Volant, Dominus, Insignia and how about Marilyn Merlot (ugh). California wineries using proprietary names are not restricted by the 75% grape requirement. Thus the winemaker is free to blend different grapes in proportions that will develop their own sought-after style and flavor.

A few years ago a group of California winemakers got together and developed a new trademarked category of wine called, *Meritage*. These are red or white Bordeaux-style blended wines that may or may not meet the 75% varietal requirement. They depend on name recognition, their style and their reputation for consistent quality. Just think of them as proprietary wines with the word, *Meritage* on the label. There are some lovely ones, though often overpriced.

California Grape Varieties

If all you've read up to now is not well fixed in your memory bank, that's okay, we can live with it. But the following eight wine grapes are the ones that California winemakers labor over the most, in order to provide us with some of the finest wines in the world. If you care about wine, you should know about these classic grape varieties.

FORE NOTES

Many of the grape names that follow are French and some of the phonetic pronunciations provided may be awkward here. For instance, Sauvignon Blanc...go ahead and say, blonk. Blahn is a bit much.

Prices: Inexpensive means under $8 for a 750 ml bottle. $8 to $14 moderate, $14 to $20 expensive and over that, very expensive. Prices are retail. It becomes arbitrary if you feel that $7 or $8 is expensive, but those who toil in the vineyards must make a buck, too.

The wine grape varieties listed in Group 1 and Group 2 are those with substantial plantings in California. There are about 25 white varieties (340,000 acres) and 33 red varieties (150,000 acres) grown in California. Group 3 varieties are recent to California and represent a change in direction for an increasing number of wineries.

GROUP 1
The Eight Most Important Grape Varieties

The Most Important Whites

Chardonnay (shar-doe-nay)—The finest dry white wine grape in the world makes the best white wine in California. Made in a variety of styles from the lean, well-balanced wines that go so well with food, to the rich, complex, oak-aged award winners that get so much attention. Look for a pleasant balance of fruit and acid with some toastiness from oak aging, and flavors of apples, pears, tropical fruits and citrus along with underlying buttery richness. Priced for every temperament from four to forty dollars. Goes well with shellfish, richer seafoods, poultry or as an anytime treat by itself. Also important in the production of sparkling wines.

In France the grape is responsible for all of the great white Burgundies. Among them, Chablis, Pouilly Fuissé, Meursault, Corton Charlemagne and the superb Montrachet. It is with treasures like these that we compare our finest Chardonnays, often most favorably. Also important as one of the classic Champagne grapes.

Sauvignon Blanc (so-veen-yohn blahn)—Excellent in California, it makes a racy, flavorful wine with good fruit, natural acidity and slight grassy notes. Second only to Chardonnay as a dry white table wine and, from the same winery it will sell for less. Often blended with some Semillon to soften and round out. Often aged in oak. When labeled Fumé Blanc, it's still Sauvignon Blanc with a fancy name. Goes wonderfully with light-sauced pastas and fish, soups and curries and before meal sipping.

In France the grape is used with Semillon in the Sauternes and Graves wines of Bordeaux. In the Loire it produces Sancerre and Pouilly Fumé.

Chenin Blanc (sheh-nan blahn)—Used extensively in California jug wines as a blend. When produced as a varietal wine and labeled Chenin Blanc, it can be finished either dry or somewhat sweet. The label should designate but here's a clue...in a regular bottle it's dry, in the tall long-necked bottle it's slightly sweet. At its best, it is clean and crisp with a charming floral delicacy. Somewhat out of favor these days. Too bad. If the winery takes the grape seriously it can be wonderful, inexpensive and a good place to start experimenting with varietal wines. Pair with light fish, chicken, sandwiches, salads and oriental dishes and, of course, as an aperitif.

In France it is the predominant grape of the Loire Valley where it produces Vouvray, Anjou, Saumur and a lot of sparkling wines which are labeled Mousseux.

Johannisberg Riesling (joe-hannis-berg reece-ling)—Also called White Riesling, it can be labeled with either or both names. The classic true German Riesling grape. In California it produces a lovely wine, sometimes, with a delicate aromatic, floral fruitiness and nice acidity. It can be made dry or in varying degrees of sweetness. Distinctive, goes well with shellfish and oriental dishes. When called Late Harvest, they are rich, sweet dessert wines. Check the label for style. You wouldn't want a Late Harvest to go with your seafood chowder. Inexpensive to moderate and readily available. Look for the tall, long necked bottle.

In France the grape is widely used in Alsace. In Germany it is the classic grape of the Rhine and Moselle wines.

The Most Important Reds

Cabernet Sauvignon (cab-air-nay so-veen-yohn)—Produces California's best red wine. Also used in other states and many parts of the world. Dry, full-bodied with aromas of violets or eucalyptus and rich, complex berry, bell pepper and black currant flavors. Firm tannins contribute to aging and recede and soften with time. Often blended with Merlot to soften and Cabernet Franc to add complexity and structure. Some are so wonderful they manifest the winemaker's art and the excellence of the grape at its most sublime. (One can get carried away.) Varying styles and quality from inexpensive to expensive. Roast duck, turkey, lamb, steak, cheddar cheese. Terrific with a Snickers bar.

In France it is the basic grape of the great chateau clarets of Bordeaux. Salivate over great names like Chateau Lafite-Rothschild, Chateau Margaux, Chateau Latour and others of equal rank and many of lesser. Fun to compare with our Cabernets, but difficult—differences in soil and climate, you know.

Merlot (mair-lo)—Increasingly important in California. Used as a softening blend in Cabernet Sauvignon and as a very nice varietal wine all its own. Soft, medium to full bodied with spicy, berry-fruit flavors and sometimes a hint of cherry. Lower tannins than Cabernets, it's drinkable sooner but not as long-lived.

Moderate to expensive. Try with stews, roasted poultry and veal and beefsteak. Well, just about anything but oatmeal.

In France it's one of the chief varieties in Bordeaux wines, acting as a softening blend in many Cabernet based wines. Predominant in the wines of Saint-Emilion with names like Chateau Ausone, Cheval Blanc and Figeac. And in Pomerol with the great Chateau Petrus, Lefleur and Trotanoy.

Pinot Noir (pee-no n'wahr)—A challenging grape for all wine-makers. California continues to improve the wine, while Oregon does quite well by it. At their best they are medium-bodied, complex and elegant, and more accessible than Cabernet Sauvignon due to lighter tannins. The good ones show delicate scents of flowers and cherry and mint flavors. Inexpensive to very expensive. Drink them with turkey, roast beef and roast pork, stews and blue and Swiss cheeses—even some highly flavored fish dishes.

In France the grape of the great red Burgundies: Romanee-Conti, Chambertin, Corton, Pommard and many others. Among the greatest wines in the world—don't even try to compare with California Pinot Noirs. Also used extensively in Champagne.

Zinfandel (zin-fan-dell)—Most acreage of any red wine grape in California, which provides the ideal soil and climate. Makes wonderful wines in many styles from light and fruity to medium bodied to robust, intense and tannic. Shows spicy, berrylike flavors and often an appealing briary character, maybe even chocolate. Also used to make White Zinfandel, a winery's bill payer. Get into them, the reds that is—they generally cost less than Cabernets and substitute well. Perfect with pastas, roast chicken, pork, sausage, lamb, veal, venison, Stilton and other sharp cheese.

Not in France. The grape is pretty much ours. Of uncertain origin, believed by many to be the Primitivo grape of south-east Italy. But not to care where it came from, you'll love the wine it makes.

GROUP 2
Eleven Less Important Grape Varieties

The following eleven grape varieties are less favored than those of Group 1, generally speaking that is, some of them poke their heads up here and there in a rather exceptional way. Pinot Blanc can be very nice and I'm especially fond of Syrah and Petite Sirah, all of which are gaining in popularity.

Less Important Whites

Pinot Blanc (pee-no-blahn)—A few California wineries bottle it as a varietal...more should, as it can produce a very nice dry wine. Also used as a blend in some California sparkling wines. Inexpensive to moderate. Some plantings in the Alsace region of France and in Germany and Italy.

Gewurztraminer (geh-vairtz-tra-mee-ner)—Fun to say, once you get the hang of it—but not always fun to drink. A difficult grape for California, but when it's done well it's delightful. *Gewurz* means spicy and *traminer* is the grape. In California it ranges from dry to varying degrees of sweetness. The sweetest are called Late Harvest. Great bouquet, pungent and perfumey. Inexpensive to moderate. Important in the Alsace region of France where it produces dry to off-dry wines. Also grown in Germany and Italy.

Semillon (seh-me-yohn)—Important in California as a softening blend in Sauvignon Blanc. Also bottled as a soft, full, dry wine all by itself. Displays pleasant fruit, but low acidity; if you're into bland this may be your wine. Inexpensive. In France it's the predominant grape in Sauternes and Graves. Also important in Australia and Chile.

Emerald Riesling—A California developed grape used in blending and also as a light, off-dry varietal wine. Paul Masson labels it Emerald Dry and was one of the first wineries to work with the grape. Inexpensive.

Grey Riesling—Not a true Riesling grape. In California it makes an inexpensive fruity off-dry light wine. Only a few wineries produce it. My first experience with the wine was many years ago, Wente Bros. was known for it.

French Colombard (cohl-om-bar)—A workhorse grape, the most widely planted white wine grape in California. Extensively used as a blend with Chenin Blanc in jug wines labeled Chablis. Bottled as a varietal it is light, fresh and slightly floral. Inexpensive. Some use in Bordeaux where it's called Colombard.

Less Important Reds

Syrah (see-rah)—Very little acreage in California but it's increasing as more wineries become interested in this true grape of France's Rhone Valley. It's also the same grape as Australia's Shiraz. We'll continue to hear more about this grape. Produces moderate to expensive wines that can be light and fruity or big and rich and long lived. Very tasty.

Petite Sirah (peh-teet see-rah)—Used for blending with lighter red wines to beef them up. But more wineries are now bottling it as a very interesting varietal. Deep and robust with spicy, sometimes peppery notes. Firm tannins give the wines aging potential. Not the same grape as the Syrah above. Inexpensive to moderate.

Gamay (gam-ay)—Known as Napa-Gamay in California, it produces a fresh, fruity wine that drinks best when young (not you, the wine). Wines labeled Gamay Beaujolais are not the same grape, but the result is so close that I wouldn't fuss over it. It's confusing enough. The true Gamay grape is very important in the Beaujolais district of France and in the Loire Valley.

Grenache (greh-nosh)—Large plantings in California go mainly to blending in jug wines. As a varietal red it is medium-bodied and pleasantly fruity. Also makes White Grenache, a light fruity pink wine. Inexpensive. Used extensively in France in Chateauneuf-du-Pape and in the famed Tavel rosés. Also important in Spain's Rioja wines.

Barbera (bar-bear-ah)—Used mostly as a blending grape in California. As a varietal it is full-bodied, fruity, often tannic and difficult to find. However, a few wineries have recently taken the grape to award winning levels. A very important grape in Italy's Piedmont region.

GROUP 3
Six Up-and-Coming Grape Varieties

With thousands of wineries here and throughout the world producing Chardonnay and Cabernet Sauvignon, there are a few forward looking California wineries seeking relief, a way out of the sameness and the fierce competition. They are experimenting with several European grape varieties that are new to this country. I've tasted a few and I think they're on to something—it's an exciting new direction but a few years away from solid answers.

The Whites

Viognier (vee-oh-n'yeh)—A rare grape producing expensive wine in France's northern Rhone Valley. And now it's gaining a roothold in California, which may have a better climate for it. Known for its fragrance of peaches and apricots.

Marsanne (mar-san)—Another Rhone grape, producing fragrant, full-bodied whites including the famed Hermitage wines. Sometimes blended with Roussanne. In California it is in the experimental stage, promising but still a puzzlement.

Roussanne (roo-sahn)—The third important northern Rhone white grape. Light and perfumey. Again, it's experimental in California as a wine on its own and also blended with Marsanne.

The Reds

Syrah (see-rah)—Also listed in Group 2. It is a very important grape in the Rhone Valley of France. Acreage is increasing in California where it shines on its own and in blends with Mourvedre and Grenache. Rich, deep colored, long-lived.

Mourvedre (moor-ved'r)—Important in the Rhone and in Provence. Deep red, rich and robust. In California it's also known as Mataro, where it does have a history and some acreage of old vines. New plantings reinforce the confidence in this grape for a stand-alone wine and as a blend with Syrah.

Nebbiolo (neh-bee-yoh-lo)—With Sangiovese, the two outstanding red grapes of Italy. Most important grape of the Piedmont region and one of the finest red grapes in the world. Makes the great Barolo, Barbaresco and Gattinara. Rich, intense and long-lived. In California the few acres of Nebbiolo are being augmented with new plantings and several producers' wines have reached the retail shelves.

Sangiovese (san-joh-vay-zeh)—The principal grape of Tuscany in Italy. Makes Chianti and the fine Brunello di Montalcino. Produces wines in varying styles from light and fruity to sturdy, rich and full. California has the climate for it and it is being planted on an experimental basis in several areas. A few wineries are in the market with their offerings with mixed results. It needs more time, but I would bet on it for the future.

California Wine Districts, Counties and Approved Viticultural Areas

Because this can become tedious, even unnecessary if gone into too deeply, I've whittled it down to some essentials which can be helpful if your knowledge of California geography is a bit shaky. I like to know where things are and I assume you do, too.

As you see on my little map of California, there are five major Wine Districts. Within these districts there are important wine producing counties. And within these counties the United States Bureau of Alcohol, Tobacco and Firearms (BATF) has defined over 56 Approved Viticultural Areas (AVAs). These grape growing areas have geographical features and climatic conditions that set them apart from surrounding areas. It's good information on a wine label because it indicates to you that the grapes come from an area especially suited to growing that variety—and it holds the promise of being a special bottle of wine.

As you read a California wine label, the most general information indicating origin of the wine would simply be—California. After that the information becomes more specific, with the name of a District or County (see below) and then, even finer, the name of an Approved Viticultural Area like Stags Leap, Howell Mountain, Carneros, Alexander Valley, etc. Certainly you won't learn all 56 but it's easy after a time to become familiar with an important few.

California
Five Wine Districts
1 North Coast
2 Central Coast
3 South Coast
4 Sierra Foothills
5 Central Valley

The 5 Districts and Their 19 Major Wine Producing Counties

North Coast—Lake, Mendocino, Napa, Sonoma, Solano.
Central Coast—Alameda, Monterey, San Benito, San Luis Obispo, Santa Barbara, Santa Clara, Santa Cruz.
South Coast—Riverside, San Diego.
Sierra Foothills—El Dorado, Amador, Calaveras.
Central Valley—Madera, Sacramento.

A Shopping List of 240 California Wines
Available • Palatable • Affordable

No one can say I don't stick my neck out. Compiling a list of quality California wines that are widely distributed and then grouping them by price is like speculating in the stock market—what's what today may not be what's what tomorrow. However, there is value in this effort for those who find shopping for wine a hit-or-miss, darn-it-I-gotta-do-it chore.

I have listed wines that you have a good chance of finding in your supermarket, local wine shop and discount or liquor store. I have listed only good, solid wineries, those that have been around a while and have earned their place in the market. Then, I have put them into price groups. Allow some leeway here, since prices will vary greatly from store to store. I'm constantly amazed at how many markets, drug and liquor stores ignore direct competition that's within a few blocks. Even cursory comparison shopping can save you enough to buy an extra bottle. And if you can get to a discount shop or warehouse club, you'll save even more.

Some wine purists may say that any wine under six or seven dollars will be of dubious quality. But a higher price does not necessarily mean better quality. Pay no 'tention, use this list as a guide to palatable wines no matter what the price. You are the judge. You taste and decide whether a $10 Chardonnay pleases you enough more than a $5 Chardonnay to be worth the difference. If not, you still have opportunities aplenty between those two prices, and above. Of course, with over 700 wineries in our golden state, I have omitted hundreds that you'd have trouble finding or those too specialized or expensive to include here. You'll ease into those later on.

California is a cornucopia of good wine. There's hardly such a thing as a bad wine. It's just that some wines are better than others and that's what you'll come to appreciate as you shop and try and taste and revel in the task.

As I've noted, things will change over time, but these wineries will survive and the price categories will remain fairly representative. The notable 1855 Classification of the red Bordeaux wines of the Medoc has changed over the last one hundred years, yet it remains usable as a guide to quality and rank. Let us hope, even though prices increase, that this list will be a helpful guide for at least the next five to ten years.

The following listings represent the wineries' regular bottlings in a standard 750 ml. size. Their higher priced special or reserve bottlings, if any, are not included.

White Wines

Chardonnay

$4 thru $7	$8 thru $12	Over $12
BV-Beautour	Beringer	Acacia-Carneros
Belvedere	Ch. St. Jean	Burgess
Callaway	Clos Du Bois	Cakebread
Fetzer-Sundial	DeLoach	Carmenet
Glen Ellen	Hess Select	Chalone
Louis Martini	Kendall-Jackson	Ferrari-Carano
Raymond-Calif.	Kenwood	Flora Springs
Round Hill	Meridian	Grgich Hills
Sebastiani	Mondavi	Jordan
Wente Bros.	Orfila Vineyards	Stags Leap
Woodbridge	Silverado	Sterling

Sauvignon Blanc and Fumé Blanc

$3 thru $4	$5 thru $8	Over $8
Bel Arbors	Beringer	Cakebread
Blossom Hill	BV-Beautour	Carmenet
Buena Vista	Chalk Hill	Guenoc
Geyser Peak	Ch. St. Jean	DeLoach
Grand Cru	Clos Du Bois	Ferrari-Carano
Napa Ridge	Dry Creek	Grgich Hills
Parducci	Fetzer	Husch
Round Hill	Kendall-Jackson	Kenwood
Sebastiani	Orfila Vineyards	Matanzas Creek
Sutter Home	Quail Ridge	Mondavi
Woodbridge	Silverado	Murphy-Goode

Chenin Blanc

$4 thru $6		Over $6
Beringer	Napa Ridge	Chalone
Callaway	L. Martini	Chappellet
Dry Creek	Parducci	Guenoc
Fetzer	Sutter Home	Kenwood
Chateau St. Michelle		Mondavi

Johannisberg/White Riesling

$4 thru $6	Over $6
Beringer	Firestone
Callaway	Kendall-Jackson
Columbia Crest (WA)	J. Lohr
Fetzer	V. Sattui
Geyser Peak	Mondavi

Sparkling Wines

Only wines made by the traditional Methode Champenoise are listed. You'll find the bulk processed Andre, Cooks, Ballatore (good), Eden Roc, Le Domaine, etc. for under $5 at most super markets.

$7 thru $9	$10 thru $15	Over $15
Ch. St. Jean	Domaine Carneros	S. Anderson
Culbertson	Domaine Chandon	Iron Horse
Gloria Ferrer	Jepson	"J" Jordan
Korbel	Mumm (Napa)	Roederer Estate
Maison Deutz	Piper Sonoma	Schramsberg
Michel Tribaut	Scharffenberger	
Wente Bros.	Shadow Ridge	

White Zinfandel—Blush/Rosé

From $4 to $8

Bel Arbors	Kenwood	Pedroncelli
Belvedere	L. Martini	Round Hill
Beringer	Paul Masson	Rutherford Estate
DeLoach	Mirassou	Sebastiani
Fetzer	Mondavi	Sutter Home
Glen Ellen	Napa Ridge	Wente Bros.
Grand Cru	Parducci	Wm. Wheeler

Red Wines

Cabernet Sauvignon

$5 thru $7	$8 thru $14	Over $14
Buena Vista	Beringer	Burgess
BV-Beautour	Benziger	Carmenet
Fetzer-Valley Oaks	BV-Rutherford	Caymus
Firestone	Chalk Hill	Chateau Montelena
Geyser Peak	Clos Du Val	Clos Du Bois-
Louis Martini	Fetzer-Barrel Select	(Marlstone)
Parducci	Kendall-Jackson	Flora Springs
Round Hill	Kenwood	Heitz-Napa
Sebastiani	Chas. Krug	Hess Collection
Vichon	Mondavi	Jordan
Wente Bros.	Raymond	Silver Oak
Woodbridge	Silverado	Stags Leap

Pinot Noir

$7 thru $10	Over $10
Acacia-Napa	Calera
Buena Vista	Chalone
Carneros Creek	DeLoach
Clos Du Bois	Mondavi
Kendall-Jackson	Morgan
Louis Martini	Saintsbury (Carneros)
Saintsbury (Garnet)	Sanford
Sonoma Creek	Wild Horse

Zinfandel (Red)

$5 thru $8	$9 thru $12	Over $12
Bel Arbors	Burgess	Clos Du Val
Beringer	Ch. Montelena	Guenoc
Fetzer	Deer Park	Kendall-Jackson
Louis Martini	DeLoach	Lytton Springs
Ravenswood-N. Coast	Grgich Hills	Rodney Strong
Round Hill	Kenwood	Mark West
Sutter Home	Meridian	Ravenswood-
Villa Mt. Eden	Ravensood-	Sonoma Valley
Woodbridge	Sonoma County	Storybook Mt.
	Ridge	Zaca Mesa

Merlot

$4 thru $7	$8 thru $12	Over $12
Beringer	Chalk Hill	Benziger
Ch. Souverain	Clos Du Bois	Clos Du Val
Fetzer	Franciscan	Cuvaison
Louis Martini	Geyser Peak	Matanzas Creek
Paul Masson	Kendall-Jackson	Newton
Round Hill	Quail Ridge	Orfila Vineyards
Sebastiani	Markham	Rutherford Hill
Stone Creek	Ravenswood	Shafer
Vichon	Wild Horse	Sterling

A Guide To The Best Years and When To Drink Them

These vintage ratings are very general. There are rating cards available at many wine shops that rate California wines by the varietal. I'm lumping all of the varietals together because what's good or bad for one varietal in a given year is often good or bad for another varietal. Not always, but close enough. There are all sorts of variables and exceptions among different grape varieties, districts and wineries. So, this is meant to be a guide, easier to remember, but not absolute. I sure covered myself on this one.

White Wines

The '87 and '88s were very good. But be wary, depending on the varietal and the winery these could be fading or gone. '89 was spotty, but there are some good ones, you'll just have to chance it. Unlikely that any will be awful. '90 and '91 are exceptional and '92 and '93 very good. They'll be your best buys.

Red Wines

The '84, '85, '86 and '87 were an exceptional run-of-four, all highly rated. In the better varietals like Cabernet Sauvignon, they will be expensive. '88 and '89 were spotty. '90 excellent and '91 and '92 are promising.

When you get right down to it, despite all protestations, California wines are very consistent from one year to another, partly due to modern vinification methods, not just the weather. Yes, there are better years than others. But that's for the experts to determine as they sniff, swirl, taste and spit. You and I, in most cases, with most wines, won't be put off with slight variations in quality. So, don't pay too much attention to the year. Just don't buy old white wine or old light reds, they may be over the hill from being around too long.

And don't worry too much about drinking a wine before its time. Most California white wines and sparkling wines are quite drinkable when they are released and only a few classy ones will get better with age. Most red wines are drinkable upon release, but many will get better with further bottle aging. Especially Cabernet Sauvignon which definitely can be drunk too soon, and Pinot Noir and Merlot to a lesser extent. You can drink white Zinfandel yesterday but red Zinfandel usually benefits by some aging.

A Potpourri of
Facts, Figures and Trivia

There are over 700 bonded wineries in California.

California produces about 90% of the wine made in the United States and about 70% of the wine consumed in the United States.

It took until 1967 for California to sell more dry wines than sweet wines. A nation weaned on Coke and Pepsi? Now it's dry by 8 to 1.

Sales of white and blush wines exceed red wine by 3 to 1. That statistic may no longer be true. Sales of red wines have surged since the "60 Minutes" report on the beneficial qualities of red wine. (*"The best glass of white wine is the first, the best glass of red wine is the last."*—Anonymous)

During prohibition (1920 to 1933) California wine production dropped from 50-million gallons to 27-million. Today California wine production is over 500-million gallons.

What is the largest winery in California, perhaps in the world? You guessed it, The E.&J. Gallo Winery in Modesto and else-where. With sales of over 50-million cases a year, their size and influence on the market is enormous. What's more, they make good wine. Not nice to sneer at brother Gallo.

• • •

The United States is one of the lowest per capita consumers of wine in the world—about 2 gallons annually, compared to 20 gallons in France and 19 gallons in Italy. Germans drink a lot of beer, also three times as much wine as we do. Obviously the U.S. consumers are not doing their part.

Italy leads the world in wine production, closely followed by France. Then Spain, Russia, the United States, Argentina and Germany, in that order. I'll bet you didn't know that Great Britain produces wine, the least of any wine producing country. But the British do consume somewhat more than we do.

• • •

California wines labeled with a year (vintage dated) must contain at least 95% of wine from that year.

Wines labeled with a varietal name (grape name) must contain a minimum of 75% of that grape.

At least 95% of a wine labeled with a vineyard name must come from that vineyard.

At least 75% of a wine labeled with a county name (Sonoma, Mendocino, etc.) must come from that county.

At least 85% of a wine labeled with an Approved Viticultural Area (Napa Valley, Alexander Valley, Temecula, etc.) must come from that area.

Legal control of the above regulations in the United States falls under the Bureau of Alcohol, Tobacco and Firearms (BATF).

Legal control in California is under the Alcoholic Beverage Control Department (ABC). And the industry is self-policed through various winery and grower associations.

Summary

Have I done my job in this chapter? After reading it do you know more about California wines, enough to make selecting wine in stores and restaurants easier, more certain and more comfortable? I think so. Especially if you will (excluding all else) give special thought and effort to learning the, "Group 1, Eight Most Important Grape Varieties" starting on page 19. If you get this section well in mind, if you experiment and maintain a continuing interest in wine, most everything else will follow.

Still, if you find yourself floundering 'midst the hundreds of wines lined up for your approval, refer to the "Shopping List of California Wines" starting on page 29. I spent hours researching and compiling this list because I thought it might be as helpful as anything I could do. Just jot down a few on your weekly shopping list. Have a couple of special wine-dinner nights—and think of me.

THE WINES OF
Other States

Featuring Our Friends To The North

Oregon and Washington are a force in grape growing and wine-making. Some very good wines, at reasonable prices, are giving California makers a run for their money. But what amazes me is that now almost every state in the nation has at least a vineyard patch somewhere. Many are of no consequence, but at least there are ground breakers out there giving it a shot.

In Illinois I spent pleasant hours sharing a bottle and much conversation with Bern Ramey who, using native American, European and hybrid grapes, made a very nice sparkling wine in the traditional methode champenoise. It was a first. John Thompson has since purchased the winery and when last I saw him was still at it. If not the only bonded winery in Illinois, it's among the very few.

Then there's a tongue-in-cheek article I once considered writing on, "Little Known Wines of America." It was to include anecdotes about such fictitious wines as Connecticut Burgundy, Tennessee Chablis, New Jersey Sherry and so on. Not so amusing now, those states and a couple dozen others are producing wines few would have thought possible back then. There's even a winery on Maui in Hawaii. After beating a path up the mountain to their winery door, they tried to charge me a dollar to use their corkscrew on a bottle I was purchasing. I let them keep their corkscrew and their bottle. Hmph!

Let's review some of the more important wine producing

states. If you live in California, or nearby, the northwest and western states are within reasonable touring distance. A stop at a winery adds to your adventure.

Northwest

Oregon—The cooler climate restricts the use of some varietals but the state is most successful with Chardonnay, White Riesling, Sauvignon Blanc, Pinot Gris and is best known for Pinot Noir. There are a number of wineries scattered along or near Route 5 going north from the California border to Roseberg. But the best are concentrated in the Willamette Valley southwest of Portland.

Some of the most notable of over 70 wineries in Oregon are: Adelsheim, Bethel Heights, Drouhin (a Burgundy producer in France trying Pinot Noir in Oregon). Elk Cove, Eyrie, Honeywood (near Salem, oldest and one of largest), Oak Knoll, Panther Creek, Ponzi (no, not a California scam), Rex Hill, Sokol Blosser and Yamhill. Some of these wines are available in California. All of them make Pinot Noir and some of them are excellent.

Washington—The climate in the grape growing areas equals that of California. And they are producing good wines that come to market at reasonable prices. Washington does well with most of the traditional vinifera varieties—Chardonnay, Sauvignon Blanc, White Riesling, Chenin Blanc, Semillon, Cabernet Sauvignon and Merlot, which may be their best grape. Pinot Noir they leave to Oregon and Zinfandel to California.

There are about 60 wineries in the state grouped mostly in two large areas—in the northwest around Seattle and in the south-central Columbia Valley, which includes the Yakima and Walla Walla appellations. Chateau Ste. Michelle near Seattle is the state's largest winery. Columbia Crest is under the same ownership. Their wines are among the most readily available Washington wines in California and represent good value. Other notable wineries include Arbor Crest, Blackwood Canyon, Canoe Ridge, Columbia, Covey Run, Hogue, Hyatt, Latah Creek, Leonetti, Quarry Lake, Silver Lake and Woodward Canyon.

Idaho—Only a handful of wineries. Ste. Chapelle in Caldwell near the Oregon border is the second largest winery in the northwest and their wines are available in California. Pintler and Rose Creek wineries make Chardonnay and Riesling.

West and Southwest

Arizona—A couple of good wineries near Tucson. In the event that you're touring that area and get curious, Sonoita makes Pinot Noir and Chenin Blanc and a good Cabernet Sauvignon. R.W. Webb makes a Cabernet, Chenin Blanc and French Colombard.

New Mexico—Over a dozen wineries in this historical wine producing state. Anderson Valley Vineyards near Albuquerque makes sound Cabernets, also Sauvignon Blanc and Muscat Canelli.

Texas—Becoming more important as a wine producing state. Especially Chardonnay, Sauvignon Blanc and Cabernet Sauvignon are successful. Llano Estacado near Lubbock is one of the state's most notable producers. Having spent over three years at air-fields in Texas during the war, part of the time at Lubbock, it's hard for me to believe that vines could prosper in that miserable climate. However, they do and I believe. Ste. Genevieve is the largest winery and most value conscious. Bell Mountain, Fall Creek, Messina Hof, Pheasant Ridge and Schoppaul Hill are others. All of this growth took place in the last twenty years, around Lubbock, Northwest of Dallas, near Fort Stockton and around Austin.

Midwest

As we move toward the midwest, there are wineries in Kansas, Iowa, Missouri, Indiana and Wisconsin. Not many but there are serious winemakers.

The two most important midwest states are Michigan and Ohio. For you transplanted midwesterners, we'll talk about them. It used to be that their wines were made from native American (labrusca) grapes. We'd have trouble with them after becoming accustomed to the European (vinifera) grapes grown in California. However, great changes have taken place as vineyards have been replanted to French-American hybrids and vinifera varieties.

It would be a marketing miracle if you could find any Michigan or Ohio wines in California. And any distributor who did provide them would be a marketing masochist. We have plenty of good stuff right 'round here.

Michigan—What can you say about the state that popularized Cold Duck? Remember that sweet, all-the-rage blend of sparkling red and white wine? That was long after my time in Michigan. As a boy growing up in the vineyard country around Paw Paw, I had my first bout with an alcoholic beverage. A bottle of Muscatel, a cheap sweet dessert wine favored by skid row types in Chicago, resulted in my best buddy and me becoming violently ill. Any further interest in wine that I may have had was put on hold. Today, the choices in Michigan wines are vastly improved.

The two major grape growing areas are in the northwest near Traverse City and in the southwest around Fennville, Paw Paw and Buchanan. Native American grapes are being replaced with French-American hybrids like Seyval Blanc, Vidal Blanc, Baco Noir and Chelois (about which I know nothing) and the viniferas Chardonnay, Johannisberg Riesling and Gewurztraminer. Some good wineries include Tabor Hill, Chateau Grand Traverse, Madron Lake Hills, L. Mawby, Warner, Fenn Valley and St. Julian.

Ohio—Before the Civil War and up to the 1900s, Ohio was the most important wine-producing state in the country. My earliest memory of an Ohio wine (some time after the Civil War) was a sparkling Catawba produced by Meiers, the largest wine company in Ohio. Actually, sparkling Catawba was made in Ohio around the mid-1800s and was the first American "Champagne."

Most wineries are in the north-central part of the state along Lake Erie. Catawba is still an important grape, along with the other natives, Concord and Niagara. Plantings of French-American hybrids and the viniferas, Chardonnay, Johannisberg Riesling and some Cabernet Sauvignon are increasing. Other wineries include Firelands (owned by Meiers), Chalet de Bonne, Grand River, Lonz, Markko and Steuk.

East and Southeast

There are wineries in many of the states in this area of the country but the following are of most interest and importance.

New York—The most wineries of any state except California and Oregon. Fifty years ago most plantings were in native American varieties (labrusca); the word "foxy" has long been used to describe the aroma of these grapes and their wines. Gold Seal and Great Western sparkling wines were at one time the popular choice for Midwest and Eastern wedding receptions. I could determine what was being poured the moment I walked into the reception room, the native American grape has such a distinctive odor.

Today plantings of French-American hybrids and the European vinifera varieties are increasing and some lovely wines are being made. The Finger Lakes region in the western third of the state and Long Island have the most wineries, produce most of the state's wine and provide the best climate for Chardonnay and Sauvignon Blanc (both excellent), Riesling and Seyval Blanc and even some classic reds like Cabernet Sauvignon, Merlot and Pinot Noir.

Prominent wineries are Bully Hill, Clinton, Finger Lakes, Glenora, Hargrave, Knapp, Millbrook, Palmer, Taylor and Wagner.

Maryland—A few small wineries make good wine from French-American hybrids and vinifera varieties. Boordy Vineyards at Hyden and Montbray Vineyard in Westminster are among the best.

Pennsylvania—Chaddsford Winery in the southeast part of the state, Naylor Winery and Allegro Vineyards, both near Harrisburg, make up the best in the state. Chardonnay, Cabernet Sauvignon and Chambourcin, a hybrid, are the principal grapes.

Connecticut—Yes, there are wineries, four as far as I can learn. The best is Crosswoods near North Stonington. They produce Chardonnay, Riesling, Pinot Noir and Merlot. Other wineries are Chamard, Hopkins and Stonington.

Virginia—Perhaps the first state to produce wine and the home of Thomas Jefferson who introduced the first vinifera varieties, unsuccessfully. Today over 40 wineries produce wines from Chardonnay, Cabernet Sauvignon, Merlot, Seyval Blanc and Vidal Blanc. Barboursville, Montdomaine, Meredyth, Piedmont, Rapidan River and Williamsburg are some of the better wineries. Most are situated in four wine producing areas—Monticello, Rocky Knob, Shenandoah Valley and Roanoke.

North Carolina—If you haven't visited the Biltmore Estate and mansion near Asheville, you've missed something. An added attraction, open to visitors, is the Biltmore Estate Winery. They make a good Chardonnay and Cabernet Sauvignon. The other winery of note is Westbend in Louisville, N.C.

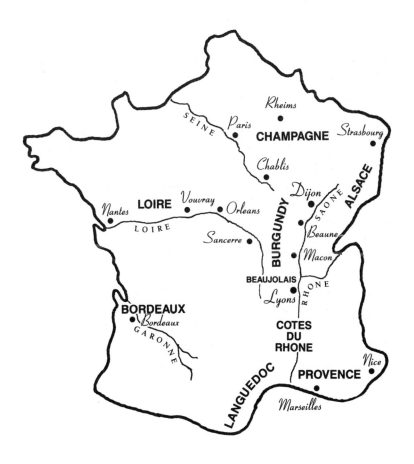

THE WINES OF

France

The Country and The People

When I think of France, I think first of the serene beauty and fascinating variety of its countryside. And then the incomparable goodness of its wines and the warmth of its people. I don't hold with the common view that the French are rude and don't like Americans. That myth has been perpetuated by those who visit Paris and feel they've visited France. Once there, they find Parisians are busy coping with urban life and, surprisingly, not everyone understands English. I'll concede that New Yorkers may not have a total monopoly on distracted busyness.

Perhaps I lived in France in another life, it agrees with me in most ways. During our many trips we have been assisted countless times when we took a wrong turn, always accommodated with fairness and honesty, befriended with warmth and spontaneity and accepted, despite language barriers, with patience and a smile.

Of course, having arrived in Paris, you must experience the history, beauty and art of the "City of Lights." Then get out—to France's endless vineyards, poplar lined canals and picturesque chateaux. Travel through villages that remain much as they were hundreds of years ago—where the pace is leisurely, the people more amiable. And, above all, partake of the passion of France, her food and wine.

Most of the wine that the French drink, and they do drink lots of it, about twenty gallons per person a year compared to our two gallons, is *vin ordinaire*. I've had a bottle or two, bought at a country market for a picnic, for a buck or two. It can test your taste buds. Our California jug wines are generally better and more consistent. But it is the other French wines that will concern us.

Growers and The Law

France has been called the world's vineyard. It produces one-fifth of the world's wine and the finest wines in the world. There are over half a million grape growers. Many produce their own wines under their own labels. Others sell grapes to negociants who make the wines and market them under their labels.

France has strict laws governing the production and labeling of wine. One of the most helpful guides for you are the words Appellation d'Origine Controlee (AOC), which appear on most of France's best wines. They simply mean, controlled place name. Knowing nothing else, these words on a wine label are your guarantee of authenticity. Everything from the geographical area, grape varieties used, allowable production per acre to the minimum alcohol content are covered by the AOC laws—sometimes simply Appellation Controlee (AC) with a place name.

Without the AOC or AC designation on a label you can be reassured by two other lesser legal classifications: Vins Délimités de Qualité Supériure (VDQS) and Vins de Pays. Both designations include some excellent wines and some very good values.

Six Most Important Wine Regions

With the brief profiles that follow, you'll have enough information to make preliminary shopping decisions within the universe of French wines. From this point it becomes a matter of your taste, what you like and what you're willing to pay for it. Each region is located for you on my little map of France.

Alsace

Alsace is located in the northeastern part of France along the Rhine River. Picturesque half-timbered houses, peaked roofs and chimneys topped with stork's nests. Incredible beauty, lush vineyards, rolling farmland, simple country food and charming wines.

The Grapes and the Wines They Make

Alsace produces mostly dry white wines. They cannot be compared with the same grape varieties used in Germany, which are finished in a lighter, slightly sweet style. There are four major grape varieties.

Riesling (reece-ling)—One of the greatest white wine grapes, some rank it above Chardonnay. Not I. In Alsace it produces a drier, more flavorful and alcoholic wine than in Germany.

Gewurztraminer (geh-vairtz-tra-mee-ner)—Gewurz means spicy and that's what it is. Dry, sometimes pungent and perfumey. They can be outstanding.

Pinot Blanc (pee-no-blahn)—An uncomplicated, pleasant dry white wine.

Sylvaner (sil-vah-ner)—Fresh, fruity and nothing not to like.

Producers

Of help in selecting a quality wine is the name of the producer or shipper on the label. A few important ones are:

J.M. Baumann	Dopff-Moulin	Albert Mann
Becker	Pierre Frick	Julien Meyer
Leon Beyer	Hugel	Schlumberger
Dopff-Irion	Kuentz-Bas	Trimbach

Summary

The wines of Alsace are easy to identify. Unlike most French wines, they are labeled with the name of the grape variety, like most U.S. wines. Look for the tall, slender-necked green bottle. The lesser wines stay in France. Most of what makes it here is quite pleasant and relatively inexpensive.

Bordeaux

Located southwest near the Atlantic coast about 300 miles from Paris, Bordeaux produces some of the finest red and white wines in the world and over one-half of the quality wines of France. It contains hundreds of chateaux, some of them mansions or grand castles, some of them simply grape farms. On a label look for the most basic appellation, *Bordeaux*. As quality increases look for the name of the district such as *Medoc*, *Pomerol* and *Sauternes*. And then the best, the individual vineyards with names of chateaux like *Chateau Lafite-Rothschild*, *Chateau Petrus* and *Chateau Climens*.

White Wines of Bordeaux

The major grape varieties are Semillon and Sauvignon Blanc. There are three major districts:

Graves (grahv)—When labeled such, produce dry wines only. When labeled Graves Superieurs, they are semi-dry. The best carry a chateau name like Chateau Carbonnieux and Chateau Olivier.

Sauternes (saw-tairn)—The district includes Barsac and could be labeled either Barsac or Sauternes. All Sauternes are sweet. The best are rich and luscious with relatively high alcohol. Grapes are picked late, overripe and affected by a mold called the Noble Rot (botrytis cinerea). See box, page 75. The best will carry a chateau name. Chateau d'Yquem is the finest, and expensive.

Entre-Deux-Mers (ahn-truh duh mair)—A large district producing good everyday dry white wines at smaller prices.

Red Wines of Bordeaux

Called clarets by the British and wonderful by us. Major grapes used are Cabernet Sauvignon, Cabernet Franc and Merlot. There are four major districts:

Medoc (meh-doc)—North of the city of Bordeaux. The most important district comprising some of the very greatest vineyards and red wines in the world. The primary grape is Cabernet Sauvignon with some blending of Cabernet Franc and Merlot. These are the wines to which we compare our California Cabernet Sauvignons. The Medoc district is divided into six wine communes as follows. (Also, see listing of the 1855 Classification for Wines of the Medoc, page 49.)

Saint Estephe (sant ess-teff)—Northernmost commune of the Medoc. Slow maturing wines, deep colored, rich in fruit and tannins. Some greats are Chateau Cos d'Estournel and Chateau Montrose.

Pauillac (paw-yack)—Classic clarets. Deep colored wines of finesse and elegance. Long-lived. Includes familiar names like Chateau Lafite-Rothschild and Chateau Latour.

Saint-Julien (san joo-l'yan)—Somewhat lighter wines than their neighbors and faster maturing. Among the top chateaux are Leoville Las Cases (my favorite) and Ducru-Beaucaillou.

Margaux (mar-go)—Southern area of the Medoc producing some of the most delicate wines. Fragrant bouquet, great elegance. Includes the first growth Chateau Margaux and Chateau Rausan Segla.

Moulis (moo-lee) and **Listrac** (lee-strawk)—The other two communes, in the southwest area of the Medoc, both produce good, moderately priced, dry, fruity wines. Earlier maturing than their grander neighbors. Excellent values.

Saint-Emilion (sant eh-mee-l'yon)—Picturesque medieval town east of the city of Bordeaux. The district produces full, rich, soft wines made predominantly with Merlot. Faster maturing then Medoc wines. The greatest are Chateau Ausone and Chateau Cheval Blanc.

Pomerol (paw-meh-rawl)—Northeast of Bordeaux. Smallest of the districts. Fuller bodied than Saint-Emilion, velvety and rich. Merlot and Cabernet Franc are the major grapes. Home to the great Chateau Petrus, one of the world's most expensive wines.

Graves (grahv)—Southwest of the city of Bordeaux. Using the same grapes but softer than the Medocs. Most famous—Chateau Haut Brion.

1855 Classification for Wines of the Medoc

I've given this much thought and have finally decided to include the controversial, 1855 Classification for the Medoc. Even though conditions have changed over the years it is still referred to as a guide to quality, ranking and price. And it can be of value to you.

The First Growths (think of Growths as meaning, Classification) are out of sight, the best vintages selling at retail for from $50 to over $100 a bottle. The Second Growths from $25 to over $60. The Third Growths are priced somewhat lower and the Fourth and Fifth Growths include some marvelous wines at more manageable prices. The trick here is to use the list to determine from which commune some of the hot shots come from and then look for that commune name on the label of some lesser Medocs. For instance, Chateau Gloria, a St.-Julien, was not classified, yet it equals and surpasses many on this list at a much lower price. All names are preceded by the word Chateau.

First Growths	Commune	Third Growths cont.	Commune
Chateaux-		Chateaux-	
Lafite-Rothschild	Pauillac	Ferriere	Margaux
Latour	Pauillac	Marquis d'Alesme-	
Margaux	Margaux	Becker	Margaux
Mouton-Rothschild	Pauillac	**Fourth Growths**	
Haut-Brion	Graves	Chateaux-	
Second Growths		Saint-Pierre	Saint-Julien
Chateaux-		Talbot	Saint-Julien
Rausan-Ségla	Margaux	Branaire-Ducru	Saint-Julien
Rauzan-Gassies	Margaux	Duhart-Milon-	
Léoville Las Cases	Saint-Julien	Rothschild	Pauillac
Léoville Poyferre	Saint-Julien	Pouget	Margaux
Léoville Barton	Saint-Julien	La Tour Carnet	Saint-Laurent
Durfort-Vivens	Margaux	Lafon-Rochet	Saint-Estephe
Gruaud-Larose	Saint-Julien	Beychevelle	Saint-Julien
Lascombes	Margaux	Prieuré-Lichine	Margaux
Brane-Cantenac	Margaux	Marquis de Terme	Margaux
Pichon-Longueville		**Fifth Growths**	
Baron	Pauillac	Chateaux-	
Pichon-Longueville		Pontet-Canet	Pauillac
Lalande	Pauillac	Batailley	Pauillac
Ducru-Beaucaillou	Saint-Julien	Haut-Batailley	Pauillac
Cos d'Estournel	Saint-Estephe	Grand-Puy-Lacoste	Pauillac
Montrose	Saint-Estephe	Grand-Puy-Ducasse	Pauillac
Third Growths		Lynch-Bages	Pauillac
Chateaux-		Lynch-Moussas	Pauillac
Kirwan	Margaux	Dauzac	Labarde
d'Issan	Margaux	Mouton-Baronne-	
Lagrange	Saint-Julien	Philippe	Pauillac
Langoa-Barton	Saint-Julien	du Tertre	Arsac
Giscours	Margaux	Haut-Bages Libéral	Pauillac
Malescot St. Exupéry	Margaux	Pédesclaux	Pauillac
Cantenac-Brown	Margaux	Belgrave	Saint-Laurent
Boyd-Cantenac	Margaux	Camensac	Saint-Laurent
Palmer	Margaux	Cos Labory	Saint-Estephe
La Lagune	Ludon	Clerc-Milon	Pauillac
Desmirail	Margaux	Croizet Bages	Pauillac
Calon-Ségur	Saint Estephe	Cantemerle	Macau

Summary

Bordeaux wines are not complicated unless one makes them so. You'll have enough information to select if you learn that...

- The best **white** wine districts are **Graves**, which are dry to semi-dry and **Sauternes,** which are sweet.

- The four major **red** wine districts are the **Medoc** (with its six important communes) then **Saint-Emilion, Pomerol** and **Graves.**

Look for those district names on the label. In the case of the Medocs the commune name, if appropriate, will also be shown. With that information your choice then is among the many chateaux, also named on the label. Here you experiment within your price range or ask for guidance from the person in charge of the wine department or the wine shop proprietor. Don't be shy about asking for help. It's expected and welcomed.

Note: A quick way to distinguish a Bordeaux from a Burgundy— most Bordeaux wine names are preceded by the word, Chateau. Burgundies seldom include the word. Also note the difference in bottle shapes. Bordeaux bottles have high shoulders starting just below the neck. The shoulder of a Burgundy bottle slopes gradually from the neck to a squatter body.

Burgundy

Located around the town of Chablis 90 miles southeast of Paris. Then skipping farther southeast starting at Dijon and south from there to Lyon. Burgundy is a region in France and only wines from this region are entitled to carry the appellation *Burgundy.* It is a wonderful area for rambling. Leave the highway and follow any country road. You may be the only one for miles as you wind through villages that overlook vineyards and their endless undulating rows of green. And then you may just happen upon the perfect place for lunch, and a bottle.

The red and white wines of Burgundy are among the finest in the world. There will always be arguments as to which of the best of Bordeaux and Burgundy are really the best of all. (Mind you, I said, best.) It is a difficult region to sort out because there are thousands of separately owned vineyards, many with important and famous names. We'll not get into the vineyards but we will mention the villages, which are a good place to start and are easier to remember. On a label, the most ordinary wine would simply be labeled, Bourgogne (Burgundy). There are three other appellations or legal classifications. Prices escalate as the quality increases.

Village Wine—Carries the village name only. Many good wines at fairly reasonable prices.

Premier Cru—Better, carries the name of a village and a specific vineyard. Expensive.

Grand Cru—The best, carrying the name of a specific vineyard only. Very expensive.

A Word About The Words, Chablis and Burgundy

Please remember that Chablis and Burgundy are wine producing areas in France. The use of those words on white and red jug wines in the U.S. started over one hundred years ago in an attempt to glamorize ordinary wines. Although the words have become accepted through long use, the wines bear no resemblance to those produced in France. They are not even made from the same grape varieties. I'd like to see it changed. It is time to let you know what you are buying.

White Wines of Burgundy

All white Burgundies are made from the Chardonnay grape exclusively. There are three districts:

Chablis (shah-blee)—A village southeast of Paris surrounded by Chardonnay vineyards. These exceptional dry white wines are full flavored and clean with crisp acidity. Most wines are simply labeled Chablis, but there are three other appellations:

Petit Chablis—Inexpensive, can be quite pleasant.

Chablis Premier Cru—Lovely, my friend, but expensive.

Chablis Grand Cru—The best. Very expensive.

Cote de Beaune (coat duh bone)—The southern half of the Cote d'Or (golden slope) just below Beaune and the Cote de Nuits. Famous for both red and white wines. The whites are superb and tend to be softer and fruitier than the crisp Chablis. Labeled Cote de Beaune-Villages they are blends from different appellations and constitute good value. There are four important appellations (village names) to look for:

Aloxe-Corton	*Puligny-Montrachet*
Meursault	*Chassagne Montrachet*

They are expensive, but there is resistance and prices are falling.

Maconnais or Macon (mah-cawn-nay)—The farthest south white wine area in Burgundy. The Chardonnay grape produces dry, fresh, palatable, good value wines. The following seven village appellations include some famous names, in order of importance:

Pouilly-Fuissé—Yes, this famous wine is all Chardonnay.

Pouilly Vinzelles

Pouilly-Loche

Saint-Veran—Inexpensive substitute for Pouilly-Fuisse.

Macon Villages

Macon Superiere

Macon—The basic, everyday wine.

Red Wines of Burgundy

Red Burgundies are made from the Pinot Noir grape only, except for Beaujolais, which is made from Gamay. There are four important districts:

Cote de Nuits (coat duh n'wee)—Northern part of the Cote d'Or below Dijon. Rivaled only by the Medoc wines of Bordeaux. The wines are full-bodied and rich with wonderful bouquet. Labeled Cote de Nuits-Villages, they are good, but less expensive blends from several village appellations. The major village appellations are:

Gevrey-Chambertin	*Vougeot*
Morey-Saint-Denis	*Vosne-Romanee*
Chambolle-Musigny	*Nuits-Saint-Georges*

Within these famed villages lie some of the world's greatest vineyards. Very expensive.

Cote de Beaune (coat duh bone)—The southern part of the Cote d'Or. Produces lighter reds than those of the Cote de Nuits, soft and charming, but they don't age quite as well. Expensive. The important village appellations are:

Aloxe-Corton   Beaune   Pommard   Volnay

Chalonnaise or Chalon (shah-loh-nez)—A district south of the Cote de Beaune. Produces wines of good quality at prices considerably less than their northern neighbors. The major villages are:

Mercury   Givry   Rully

Some good values here to introduce you to red Burgundy.

Beaujolais—It's bo, not boo. In the southern part of Burgundy below Macon. The most popular wine in France—it flows like water. Light and fruity, it is made from the Gamay grape. There are three quality designations. The basic wine is simply labeled, Beaujolais. The next highest is Beaujolais Villages and the best are the ten classified crus:

Brouilly	*Cote de Brouilly*	*Morgon*
Chenas	*Fleurie*	*Moulin-a-vent*
Chiroubles	*Julienas*	*Regnie*
	Saint-Amour	

These wines have more intense flavors and will last longer than lesser Beaujolais. They're fine drinking and affordable.

Summary

Now, that's about as simple an outline of the wines of Burgundy as I can manage and still impart useful information.

There is enough here to guide you into a wine adventure that could bring great enjoyment. Jot down a few of the village names before you visit the Burgundy section of your local wine merchant or market. Another great help is to become familiar with some of the reliable producers like Henri Jayer, Robert Arnoux, Louis Jadot, Joseph Drouhin, Jaffelin Labouré-Roi and Louis Latour. Those names will pop right out at you from the labels.

The wines of Chablis, Maconnais, Chalonnais and Beaujolais are the easiest to shop for, less expensive and the ones you are most likely to become involved with. So, I suggest you start with them. If a thoughtful relative leaves you a fortune, try a Montrachet (white) from the village appellation Chassagne-Montrachet. And a Romanee-Conti (red) from the village appellation Vosne-Romanee. You will have enjoyed what few people ever experience—the very best Burgundies. However, you may prefer to settle for a winter cruise.

Champagne

Located in the famous sparkling wine region, 90 miles northeast of Paris. The most important areas are around the towns of Rheims, Epernay and Avize. Only sparkling wine is produced in the Champagne region of France, and only by the methode champenoise. The label will say, Champagne (if it's not from Champagne it's not Champagne). Villages, districts and vineyard names are not a factor as in some other French wines. The name of the house (producer) is what you look for.

The Grapes and The Wines They Make

Only three grapes may be used, the white Chardonnay and two reds—Pinot Noir and Pinot Meunier. All three grapes may be blended to produce a white or rosé sparkling wine. When labeled Blanc de Blancs, meaning white wine from white grapes, it is made from Chardonnay only. When labeled Blanc de Noirs, meaning a white wine from black grapes, either Pinot Noir,

Pinot Meunier, or both are used. The more Chardonnay used, the lighter the style of Champagne. Those made with the red grapes are creamier and richer.

Vintage and Non-Vintage

Vintage wines are the most expensive. They must be made from grapes of a single year. Only the best years are declared vintage years by the houses. They can be wonderful, the best in the world. Unfortunately, many of the luxury bottlings (Dom Perignon, for example) are very expensive.

Non-Vintage wines, wines without a year on their label, are the place for you to start. They are less expensive than vintage wines and can be excellent. They are wines blended from different years and vineyards to achieve a desired house style and consistency.

Degrees of Dryness

Some terms of dryness or sweetness on a bottle of Champagne can be confusing.

Extra or Ultra Brut means bone dry, no sugar added.

Brut means dry. It can have up to 1.0% sugar, but will still taste dry.

Extra Dry may have up to 2.0% sugar added. It can fool your taster. What seems to be richness and fruitiness may be the result of the slight sweetness. Nothing wrong with that.

Sec means dry, but it isn't.

Demi-Sec means medium dry, but you'll taste it as quite sweet.

When to Drink

Now, buy 'em and drink 'em. Some of the vintage dated wines and luxury bottles will improve with proper storage, but why chance it? Champagne is especially sensitive to light and temperature change. Sticking it away on a closet shelf for a year or two is risky.

Another When to Drink

Anytime. Champagne is versatile. It can be drunk before, during or after a meal, as well as upon rising and at bedtime, with pleasant results.

Major Champagne Houses

All make vintage and non-vintage wines and are available in the U.S.

Bollinger	Lanson	Pol Roger
Bricout	Laurent-Perrier	Pommery
Charbaut	Moet & Chandon*	Louis Roederer*
Charles Heidsieck	Mumm*	Ruinart
Jacquart	Perrier-Jouet	Taittinger*
Krug	Piper Heidsieck*	Veuve-Cliquot

*These French houses also have vineyards and wineries in California and are producing very nice sparkling wine in the traditional methode champenoise. You will not find the word Champagne on their California labels.

Summary

There are many very good California sparkling wines, but if you want the real thing, it has to be Champagne. Try a non-vintage Champagne, they are available at prices that start at the high end of California sparkling wine prices. What is fun is to buy a non-vintage Champagne like Moet & Chandon, then buy their California counterpart, Domaine Chandon, and compare them. They are different, as different as the soil and the climate, even though they are made the same way.

Loire Valley

Located one hundred miles south of Paris following the Loire River northwest through Orleans and on west to Nantes near the Atlantic coast. One of the loveliest areas of France, the Loire Valley has a mystical light that has attracted artists for generations. A canvas of rolling farmland, vineyards and fairytale chateaux. The place of Joan of Arc and the retreat of kings and queens. All of this and wine, wine as diverse and charming as any in France— not the greatest, not the most complicated, but certainly some of the most pleasant, approachable and affordable.

The Major Grapes

Dry white wines predominate, the major grapes being Sauvignon Blanc, Chenin Blanc and Muscadet. For red wines, Cabernet Franc, Gamay and Cabernet Sauvignon are used. There are sparkling wines that equal some of the best anywhere. And then there are the rosés, not always the best.

White Wines of The Loire

Sancerre (sahn-sair)—A village and a wine, south of Paris on the banks of the Loire. Dry, white wines made from the Sauvignon Blanc grape. Fresh, lively, delightful. Popular in France, available here.

Pouilly Fumé (poo-yee foo-may)—Across the Loire from Sancerre. Made from Sauvignon Blanc as are California wines called Fumé Blanc. Not to be confused with Pouilly Fuissé which is a Burgundy wine made from Chardonnay. Light and fruity with pleasant grassy notes.

Vouvray (voo-vray)—Despite its popularity, I have trouble with this wine. Made of Chenin Blanc, it can be dry, sort of sweet or cloyingly sweet, (often the label doesn't specify) and I don't care for the surprise. Maybe the best way to drink any untried

Vouvray would be before a meal. If it fits the food, continue with it. Also makes a fine sparkling wine called Mousseux.

Muscadet (mus-cah-day)—All the way west near Nantes. The Muscadet grape gets its name from a slight musky aroma. Dry and pleasant, they're most agreeable with seafood, especially shellfish. Popular and inexpensive.

Savennieres (sah-ven-yair)—A village southwest of Angers making some of the best dry white wine of the Loire. Made from the Chenin Blanc grape, the flavors are full and flowery, almost pungent.

Red Wines of The Loire

Bourgueil (boor-guy)—A village in the provence of Touraine where these very pleasant dry, light wines are produced. Cabernet Franc is the grape. The wine is popular in France and available here with a search.

Chinon (shee-nohn)—In the Touraine area southeast of Saumur. I drink Chinon when I'm in the Loire; I love it. But with great absence of mind I've never had it here—an oversight soon to be corrected. Made from Cabernet Franc, it is the best of the Loire reds. Rich, ripe and smooth with berry flavors and enough structure to provide some aging.

Rosés of The Loire

Rosé d'Anjou (ro-zay dahn-joo)—A pink wine of some fame from the Anjou area. Made slightly sweet primarily from the Gamay and Groslot grapes.

Cabernet d'Anjou—A semi dry rosé made from Cabernet Franc and usually preferable to the Rosé d'Anjou.

Rosé de Loire—A general appellation for dry rosé wines of the Loire Valley. Made from several grapes, Cabernet Franc being dominant. Made in a variety of styles.

Sparkling Wines of The Loire

They are usually made by the methode champenoise, are fully sparkling and labeled with the word Mousseux. The word Cremant is applied to those wines that have somewhat less sparkle than the Mousseux. Either can be excellent, cost less and give some good Champagnes a run for your money. I remember a bottle of Vouvray Mousseux at Le Prieure, near Saumur on a rainy fall evening. It made our anniversary dinner a bit more special.

Summary

The Loire Valley is a vast wine-making area, but to me, not nearly so complicated as Bordeaux or Burgundy. The wines are usually modestly priced but often difficult to find in the U.S. The dry white and red wines are excellent. Try a Mousseux sparkling wine. But I do not suggest the Loire rosés; the Tavels from the Rhone region are better. Finally, the Loire is yet another good vineyard in a world of good wine.

Cotes du Rhone
And A Few Words About Provence

Located in the Rhone Valley in the southeastern part of France, below Burgundy, between Vienne on the north and Avignon on the south. Lots to see and do in the Rhone Valley. Sturdy wines, sturdy food, sturdy souls. Very rural, great stretches of vineyards, Roman ruins, ancient villages, tranquility and warmth. Some of the heartiest, most likable wines of France, they are bigger, fuller and more alcoholic than Burgundies, and mostly less expensive. The valley is divided into the north half and the south half and, although they make different wines, we'll ignore the distinction and just talk about Rhone wines.

The Major Grapes

Several varieties of grapes are used but the most important reds are Grenache and Syrah. The whites include Marsanne, Roussanne, Grenache Blanc and, increasingly, Viognier.

Red Wines of The Rhone

Cote Rotie (coat-roe-tee)—Fine reds. Spicy, deep colored and they are rich. Big full-bodied wines made from the Syrah grape. They'll age well. Expensive.

Cornas (cor-nahss)—Among the most robust red wines you're likely to run across. Made from the Syrah, they develop powerful berry aromas and flavors and become more complex with age. Moderately priced and delicious.

Hermitage (air-mee-tahj)—Some of the best reds in France. Deep colored, rich and full-bodied. Made from the Syrah grape. They'll age well and they are expensive.

Crozes Hermitage (crawz air-mee-tahj)—The reds, made from Syrah, are similar to the nearby Hermitage but they are not as rich and they won't age quite as long. Moderately priced.

Chateauneuf-du-Pape (shah-toe-nuff doo pahp)—Means, the new castle of the Pope. In the fourteenth century it was the summer home of the Avignon Popes which is now in ruins. The vineyards lie in the southern half of the Rhone near Avignon. One of France's most famous wines and for good reason. Although not as big as the reds listed above, they are soft, tasty and easy drinking. Thirteen different red and white grapes are allowed but Grenache and Syrah predominate. Made in many styles at many price levels, they're available in most stores and in many restaurants. As approachable as they are, they age fairly well. There's one out there for you and I think you should go for it. A small percentage of whites are made from the Clairette grape and they're pretty good.

Cotes du Rhone and Cotes du Rhone-Villages (coat doo rone vee-lahj)—Cotes du Rhone is a general name for all of the Rhone Valley wines. They are less prestigious than those that also carry a vineyard or district name. Those labeled Cotes du Rhone-Villages are a cut above. Both nomenclatures include red, white and rosé wines in a diversity of styles and qualities. Some twenty grape varieties are allowed. Grenache and Syrah (reds) and Marsanne (white) predominate. I've consumed many a bottle and many are very good indeed. Reasonably priced and available, they represent good value.

White and Rosé Wines of The Rhone

Condrieu (con-dree-uh)—An unusual white wine made from the rare but increasingly planted Viognier grape. It is packed with rich fruit flavors and floral aromas. If you can find one, let's try it together. Soon, since they don't age particularly well. A bit expensive due to its rarity. I've mentioned it because you'll be hearing more about the grape.

Hermitage (air-mee-tahj)—In addition to its fine reds, the area produces fine whites made from the Marsanne grape. Full-bodied and powerful, here's a white that ages well. Expensive.

Crozes Hermitage (crahz air-mee-tahj)—Besides the reds the area makes a fine white that's lighter and less complex than the Hermitage. Costs less, too. Marsanne's the grape.

Tavel (tah-vel)—France's best and most famous rosé. Across the river from Chateauneuf-du-Pape west of Avignon. Made primarily with Grenache and some Cinsault. They are agreeably fruity and dry with a pink-orange tint. Pretty good for a rosé and not expensive.

Summary

The wines of the Rhone, once overlooked by the American wine consumer, are becoming more popular. And they deserve it. Put aside the big Cote Rotie and Hermitage wines and take some chances on a modestly priced Cotes du Rhone or Cotes du Rhone-Villages. One of my favorites is the red, La Vieille Ferme. It's widely available and when properly priced runs under $6. Twenty years ago I paid $24 a case. It's still a great value at today's prices. There are others in the stores and they will help make tomorrow night's meal a special one.

A Few Words About
Provence

Provence is an ancient and intensely interesting part of France. Situated below the Rhone and east along the southern coast, the area produces a tremendous quantity of light rosé wines, some very good reds and a few whites.

I mention Provence because their wines are becoming more recognized. Wine writers and promoters are talking more about them and they do represent good value. There are seven appellations or major wine producing areas and these names will appear on the bottle labels. All produce red, rosé and white wines.

Cotes de Provence	*Bellet*
Cotes des Baux	*Cassis*
Bandol	*Palette*
Coteaux d'Aix-en-Provence	

THE WINES OF
Italy

Warm People, Rich Wines
and Food to Match

I made such a big fuss about France that much of the hyperbole is used up. I guess it's best said that Italy is totally ripe, bountiful and agreeable. The people are warm and generous, though scary behind the wheel of a car. The countryside is old and beautiful, the cities old and a mess. The food is superb from the simplest roadside trattoria to the finest three-star ristorante. And some of their red wines are as rich and voluptuous as the best in the world.

Italy makes more wine than any other country. It has been said, "there is no country, it is one vast vineyard from north to south." They make millions of gallons of indifferent bulk wine and good wine and then they make some magnificent wines that are recognized the world over for quality and longevity. What's more, Italians manage to consume more of it than anyone but the French.

There are twenty major wine regions, dozens of provinces, thousands of different wine labels and an enormous number of grape varieties. This has discouraged those who found it difficult to get beyond the straw-covered Chianti bottle. We shall attempt to overcome this problem.

The quality of Italian wines, as in France, is controlled by law. The words, Denominazione di Origine Controllota (DOC) on a bottle is your assurance that important minimum standards have been met in producing the wine. Almost all Italian wines are labeled as to their place of origin or the grape variety. They are easy to find in shops and restaurants in the U.S. and are available in many styles and qualities at prices ranging from inexpensive to very expensive.

Important Red Wine Regions

We start with Italy's red wines because they are better and more important than the white wines. I have reduced the twenty wine producing regions to just three—Tuscany, Piedmont and Veneto. Don't feel shorted, these regions include most of the great names in Italian wine. Remembering a few of them is all you'll need to drink and dine well. There are two other regions that should be noted—Trentino-Alto Adige in the north and Friuli-Venezia Guila in the northeast, but you would have great difficulty in finding their wines here.

Tuscany

Located in the west-central area around and below Florence, the principal grape used is *Sangiovese* (san-joe-vay-seh).

Chianti—The most important of Italy's controlled (DOC) wines. You'll seldom see the straw-covered (fiasco) bottle anymore—too expensive; also it continued the unwanted image of a cheap red wine. Today Chianti is available in many styles at many prices and in Bordeaux shaped bottles, yet. There are three quality levels. Among all levels there are very good, good and not so good wines. Chianti does have a reputation for inconsistency, but I always assume what they ship to us is not going to be awful. In Italy it's another matter.

Chianti—The basic quality level. Fresh, fruity and tart, medium-bodied, made to drink young. The cafe wine of Florence and most Italian restaurants in the U.S. Inexpensive.

Chianti Classico—Wines from a restricted area, implying the best. A cut above—riper, fuller, more balanced. Some aging. Inexpensive to moderate.

Chianti Classico Reserva—Classico designated wines with aging requirements of three years. Soft and rich with complex flavors and often some touches of oak. Moderate to expensive.

Brunello di Montalcino (mon-tahl-chee-no)—Among Italy's finest. Stronger, fuller than Chianti. Long-lived. Must have three and one half years of wood aging. Moderate to expensive.

Vino da Tavola—Means Table Wine. Long used name for the most ordinary wines. Now however, some of the more venturesome winemakers in Tuscany are making specialty wines from 100% Cabernet Sauvignon or Sangiovese or blends of Cabernet Sauvignon, Sangiovese, Cabernet Franc or Merlot. Because of legal restrictions on the use of grape varieties, they use proprietary label names, as do our California Meritage wines. When you see a wine label with the Tuscany designation that lists grape varieties other than Sangiovese you've probably found one of the new Vino da Tavola wines. Expensive.

Piedmont

Located in the northwest, surrounding the city of Turino, the principal grapes used are *Nebbiolo, Barbera* and *Dolcetto.*

Barolo (bah-roe-low)—Considered the king of Italian wine. Made from the Nebbiolo grape, it is big, robust, tannic and long-lived. At their best they just burst with flavor and aroma. They're often drunk too soon. In a restaurant I'm leery of any that are under six years old and I'd prefer nine or ten. However, help is on the way as Piedmont winemakers have begun producing Barolos that are rich and ripe with softer tannins. The fine 1988, '89 and '90 are good examples of this gathering change to more accessible, earlier drinking wine. Moderate to very expensive.

Barbaresco (bar-bah-ress-co)—Made from the Nebbiolo grape. Traditionally softer and lighter than Barolo and requiring less aging. Dry, velvety, intensely fruity. If the Barolo in a restaurant is too young, I switch to a Barbaresco. However, as with the Barolos, the 1988, '89 and '90 Barbarescos are examples of the new thinking in Piedmont. They'll be in top drinking form sooner than some of the older vintages. Moderate to very expensive.

Barbera (bar-bear-ah)—Made from the Barbera grape. Dry, strong, tangy. The best having great fruit and body. They drink better with a few years of age. Inexpensive to moderate.

Gattinara (gat-in-ara)—Made from the Nebbiolo. Not as rich or complex as Barolo or Barbaresco but a softer, fruitier, less expensive substitute if you'll give up some class.

Dolcetto (dole-chet-oh)—Made from the Dolcetto grape. Named for its sweet juice, however, it is always finished dry. A delightful wine, soft, rich and eminently drinkable. Chianti can be disappointing; you're safer with this wine if you drink it young, under three years. Inexpensive.

Note: Several times I have found good Barolos and Barbarescos in discount wine shops for less than $12 (how do they do it?) Having been pleased with the quality for the price, I suggest taking a chance on them.

Veneto

Located northeast near Venice and Verona, the principal grapes used are *Corvina, Rondinella* and *Molinare.*

Bardolino (bar-doe-lee-no)—In many Italian restaurants and markets in the U.S. Light, fruity and pleasant. Made from all three grapes above. Lower alcohol than Piedmont reds. Most agreeable with everyday dining. Best drunk young, be wary of any over five years of age. Inexpensive.

Valpolicella (val-poh-lee-chella-ah)—Fuller and richer than the Bardolino, though made from the same grapes. Finding the two on a wine list, I'd select the Valpolicella. Pleasant, fruity and fragrant. Drink it young. Inexpensive. Those labeled Valpolicella Classico or Superiore are a big cut above the regular bottle—richer, fuller, more alcoholic and pricier.

Important White Wines

The production of good red wines is concentrated in a few regions but the significant white wines come from more scattered areas. So I'll just compile the list alphabetically and give you a quick idea of where they're from and what they are. You'll be familiar with many of the names. Many are on restaurant lists and sometimes dreadfully overpriced.

Asti Spumante—Spumante means sparkling. From Piedmont, near the village of Asti, the grape is Moscato di Canelli. Makes a sweet, grapey, low alcohol sparkler. More are making it now in a dry style from traditional grapes like Chardonnay. I'd suggest the latter, not the sweet ones. Inexpensive.

Est! Est!! Est!!! (di Montefiascone)—Light, dry simple wine grown north of Rome. Made from Trebbiano and Malvasia grapes. Its unusual name is about its only claim to fame. Way back in the twelfth century a wine-imbibing German bishop set out for Rome. Not wanting to chance the local wines he sent his servant ahead to scout and taste. If the wine at a particular tavern was good, he was to write Est (it is) on the wall. At the village of Montefiascone he wrote, Est! Est!! Est!!! As the legend goes, the bishop liked the wine so much he lived out his life there. Each year the town is supposed to pour a barrel of wine over his grave. Believing all of that might make the wine more palatable.

Frascati (frahs-cah-tee)—Pleasant, dry, light bodied wine from south of Rome. I've partaken of many a good bottle over there but I've learned it should be drunk very young over here. Try it if it's less than three years old. Inexpensive.

Lacryma Christi (lah-cree-ma kriss-tee) *Tears of Christ*—Produced on the slopes of Vesuvius near Naples from three native grapes.

Flowery scent, delicate flavor, somewhat sweet. Inexpensive. Often overpriced in U.S. restaurants because of the name, I suppose.

Orvieto (ore-v'yay-toh)—Pleasant, light and delicate. Made from Trebbiano and Verdello grapes, near the wonderful ancient village of Orvieto in the Umbria region. Most are dry, some made semi-sweet. Inexpensive.

Pinot Grigio (pee-no gree-d'jo)—From the Pinot Gris grape widely planted in the northern part of Italy. The best are dry, light and flavorful. I like the perception of crisp acidity in the good ones. Those with the name Santa Margherita have more body, fruit and character, but at the price on most lists I'd opt for the less expensive one.

Soave (s'wah-vey)—Produced near Verona of Gargenega and some Trebbiano. The most important and one of the best Italian whites. Dry, light-bodied and fresh. They're on many wine lists and in most markets in the U.S. Better today than they used to be. I like them when they taste a little zingy. Inexpensive.

Verdicchio (vair-dik-ee-oh)—From the Marches region south-east of Florence on the Adriatic. Verdicchio is the major grape with some Trebbiano or Malvasia. Famous for its graceful, green, amphora-shaped bottle. Today, also in regular bottles. Clean, dry, light-bodied with light floral aromas. One of my younger-day favorites with cioppino and light-sauced pastas. Inexpensive to moderate.

Vernaccia di San Gimignano (vair-nah-t'chah dee san-jee-meen-yah-no)—The grape is Vernaccia, the village is San Gimignano in Tuscany near Florence, a fabulous ancient walled and towered fortress. And this wine, drunk there at a restaurant within the walls, was almost as delightful as the company. Considered Tuscany's best white, I remember it as fresh, fruity, of some body, with good balance between fruit and acid. Hard to find here so, let's just return to *it*!

Chardonnay and Sauvignon Blanc—Don't overlook these two classic grapes. More is being produced in Tuscany, Piedmont and other regions. They're in many markets and on wine lists in the U.S. Usually well made, usually priced reasonably because the U.S. product keeps them in line.

Producers of Italian Wines

A producer's name on a bottle is important, their reputation is at stake. There are hundreds. Some of the major producers with good reputations are:

Allegrini	Fontana Candida	Nozzole
Anselmi	Fontannafredda	Pio Cesare
Antinori	Frescobaldi	Poliziano
Bertelli	Angelo Gaja	Renato-Ratti
Biondi-Santi	Bruno Giacosa	Ruffino
Bolla	Lungarotti	Seghesio
Ceretto	Massarello	Vietti
Conterno	Monsanto	Villa Banfi

Summary

The white wines of Italy are usually modest, everyday drinking wines and should be priced accordingly in stores and restaurants. The reds can be sensational and the best are often very expensive. If you haven't been into Italian reds, I suggest you start with Dolcetto, Bardolino or Valpolicella. Then move on to the Chianti Classicos and Barbera. You may never have to reach the expensive Barolos and Barbarescos. Incidentally, early on I learned that I'd remember the Italian reds better if I got the four B's in mind as the Best—*Barolo, Barbaresco, Barbera* and *Brunello*. Kind of catchy.

I lived for many years in an area of family run Italian restaurants, knew the families, loved their food and learned about their wines. It surprises me that all of a sudden the U.S. seems to have discovered that Italian food is more than spaghetti and meatballs. If you are one who must have your, "Italian-food-fix" periodically you know that Italian food and wine go together. Their lusty, well-seasoned meats, poultry, pastas and sauces are perfectly complemented by wines of the same heft. To eat and drink Italian is one of the gustatory pleasures of life.

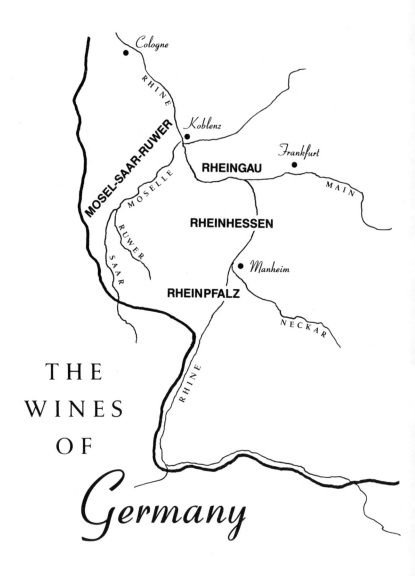

THE
WINES
OF
Germany

Some Attitudes

Just as France and Italy have been described as beautiful, so must Germany. It is difficult to imagine another vineyard area on earth that can match the breathtaking beauty of the vineyards that cushion the steep slopes along the Moselle and Rhine rivers. And then it is difficult to imagine any country that has done less to uncomplicate, and make accessible, the product of those slopes.

I confess that the subject of German wine has not been a major concern of mine. I have not concentrated on them, I have trouble selecting from what is available and then I have a devil of a time pairing them with anything except Oriental food. Another thing, why is it Germans, with all of this wonderful wine, drink more beer? For that matter, why do we?

Frankly, and this will be heresy for many devotees, I believe German wines hold a relatively unimportant place in the world of wine. Some of their marvelous dessert wines are incomparable and the delicacy of their best Rieslings is difficult to match—but the former are almost oddities and the latter are replaceable. The trouble for us is that we can't know everything. Our object is to keep this wine learning manageable. I do believe basic information on German wines is desirable so you can make up your own mind. What follows is broad enough to give you good understanding of what's going on without becoming overly involved. Actually, I think it will be quite interesting.

The Grapes

Most German wine is white and low in alcohol. The reds are not worth mentioning. Many knowledgeable wine folk believe the finest German white wines are among the best in the world. Three major grape varieties are used. By far the most important is Riesling, it is the king, accounting for most of Germany's finest wine. Muller-Thurgau and Sylvaner are two others grown in quantity. And there is some Gewurtztraminer.

Quality Designations

The quality of German wines is controlled by a set of 1971 laws and provides for the following three quality designations. This is important information on a German wine label.

Tafelwein (tah-fel-vine)—Means table wine. The lowest quality. Uncommon in the U.S.

Qualitatswein (or QbA) (kval-ee-tates-vine)—Means quality wine. Must be made from grapes containing a specified amount of natural sugar and must come from one of several specified regions. Look for this word on the bottle.

Qualitatswein mit Pradikat (or QmP) (pray-dee-kat)—Quality wine with special attributes. Designated on the label as follows:

Kabinett (kah-bee-net)—Driest of all. Inexpensive.

Spatlese (sh-pate-lay-zuh)—Means late picking. Richer, sweeter and higher priced.

Auslese (ouse-lay-zuh)—Means selected picking. Made from selected bunches of grapes with specified sugar content. A dessert wine. Richer, sweeter, more expensive than Spatlese. May be botrytis affected, see box.

Beerenauslese (bear-en-ouse-lay-zuh)—Grapes selected individually for over-ripeness. Rich dessert wines. Rare, very expensive. Usually botrytis affected.

Trockenbeerenauslese (or TBA) (traw-ken-bear-en-ouse-lay-zuh)—You can do it! Think auselese, add beeren in front of it, then add Trocken in front of that. Specially selected grapes left on the vines until shriveled dry. Concentrated, sweet and luscious. Seldom made. Very expensive. Usually botrytis affected.

Eiswein (ice-vine)—Pressed from frozen grapes. Creates a very different sweet wine of great elegance. Very expensive.

Botrytis Cinerea
(bo-try-tiss sin-eh-ray-ah)

Otherwise known as the noble rot. Under certain climatic conditions mold forms on the skins of overripe grapes, shriveling them and reducing water content. Sugar is concentrated and the wine takes on a rich, complex, honeyed flavor. The German Auslese, Beerenauslese and Trockenbeerenauslese are usually affected. The best French Sauternes are made from botrytised grapes, as are some California wines labeled Late Harvest.

Major Wine Regions

There are eleven specified wine-making regions and one or another will appear on the wine label. We deal with the four most important.

Mosel-Saar-Ruwer (mo-zl sahr roo-ver)—Located along the Moselle (Mosel) River and its tributaries, the Saar and the Ruwer. Delicate and fragrant wines made primarily from the Riesling grape.

Rheingau (rine-gao)—West of Frankfurt along the Rhine (Rhein) River. Considered by many to be among the finest whites in the world. Not as delicate as Moselles, somewhat richer and fuller with more structure. Riesling is the grape.

Rheinhessen (rine-hess-en)—Below the Rheingau along the Rhine and inland west. Produces large quantities of ordinary wines such as, Liebfraumilch (Blue Nun and Black Tower) from primarily Muller-Thurgau and Sylvaner grapes. Also produces excellent Rieslings.

Rheinpfalz (rine-faltz)—Below the Rheinhessen east from the Rhine River south to the Alsace region of France. The best Rieslings are richer, fuller than the Rheingaus. Muller-Thurgau, Sylvaner and several other varieties are used extensively. Famous for the rare Beerenauslese wines.

Reading A German Wine Label

Look for this information on a wine label:

Region—Mosel-Saar-Ruwer, Rheingau, etc.

The Grape—The best are made from Riesling. The name will appear on the label if it makes up 85% or more of the wine.

Quality Designation—For instance, Qualitatswein mit Pradikat and any special attributes such as Kabinett or Spatlese.

The Importer—There are three major importers of German wines. It will comfort you to see one of these names on a label—Bob Rice of Chapin Cellars, Terry Theise Selections and Rudy Weist ILNA Selections.

Summary

German wine labels are easier to read than they used to be, a big step forward in marketing German wines. Generally the wines are delicate, flowery and slightly sweet and go with light dishes and Oriental food. If you're not familiar with German wines I suggest you try a bottle or two; they may be just your cup of wine. Start with an inexpensive Kabinett then, by all means, try a Spatlese. The great, rich, sweet Ausleses should be considered as dessert wines.

Moselles come in tall slender green bottles and are lighter than Rhine wines. The richer, fuller Rhines come in slender necked brown bottles.

Note: Mosel and Rhein are the German spellings of Moselle and Rhine.

THE WINES OF

Spain

Images, Memories and Information

Few have done more to create an image of Spain than Hemingway. We think of bullfights on a late Sunday afternoon, lovely senoritas and swirling skirts, tapas and red wine at a local bar in Madrid. Now weave your own memories and feelings against that background. Include the sensuous excitement of Spain's treasured art, music and dance. The fascination of ancient cities like Granada, Seville, Cordoba, Toledo, Valencia and Barcelona. Their grand cathedrals, mosques, paradors and palaces. And the countryside with acres of olive groves and vast vineyards stretching away in the hot sun. Spain is truly a feast for the senses.

Spain has more acres of vineyards than any other country, yet they are lower yielding and produce much less wine than France or Italy. Some of Spain's reds are outstanding, ranging from pale, light-bodied wines to full, rich, high alcohol wines. There are some good whites and their Espumosos, sparkling wines, are accepted the world over. Of course, Sherry is their most famous wine.

The name of the producer on a Spanish wine label is important information. But the vintage is less so—uniformity of climate reduces year to year variances. Also, wood aging of the red wines makes them more accessible, more drinkable at the time you receive them.

As in France and Italy the overall quality of wines is controlled by a set of laws known as Denominacion de Origen. Those words will appear on the label, taking some of the guesswork out of selecting a properly made wine.

Three Important Wine Regions

Rioja
(ree-oh-ha)

Located in the north central part of Spain near the French border. Rioja is Spain's most famous wine and has been since Roman times. The style of their wines is influenced somewhat by the French who, in the 1800s, left their Phylloxera ruined vineyards, crossed the Pyrenees and took up winemaking in Rioja. Most later returned to start anew in Fránce.

Red Wines of Rioja

There are two major grapes: Tempranillo and Garnacha (Grenache). The wines are lighter, softer and easier drinking than other Spanish reds. They are easy to understand, too— no classification system to learn and, in most cases, no grape varieties are listed on the label. Aging potential is over 20 years. Look for the word, Rioja, or the longer aged Rioja Riservas, and the name of the producer. Many are modestly priced and excellent values. Some of the best producers are:

Marques de Riscal

Lopez de Heredia

Marques de Murrieta

Marques de Caceras

Franco-Espanolas

Bodega Bilbainas

Frederico-Paternina

White Wines of Rioja

The major grapes—Viura and Malvasia. Made in a variety of styles. Although not broadly distributed in the U.S., those you find will be dry, light in fruit and medium to full-bodied. Some of the best producers are:

Marques de Riscal

Marques de Caceras

Marques de Murrieta

Bodega Montecillo

Penedes
(peh-neh-dess)

Located in the region near Barcelona in the northeastern corner of Spain. Penedes is an increasingly important wine producing area, making good reds, whites and the popular Espumoso sparkling wine. Two-thirds of their production is in white wines, much of which becomes Espumoso. The most important name in wine production is Torres.

Red Wines of Penedes

The major grapes are Garnacha, Tempranillo, Carinena and, increasingly, some Cabernet Sauvignon and Merlot. Penedes reds have reached a level of quality equaling the best Riojas. They tend to be richer and fuller wines and are good values. Aging potential up to 15 years. Look for the region name, Penedes, on the label and the name of the producer. Some of the best producers are:

Masia Bach	*Raimat*
René Barbier	*Jaume Serra*
Scala dei Priorato	*Torres*

White Wines of Penedes

The major grapes are Xarello, Macabeo, Parellada and some good ole Chardonnay. Among the best white wines in Spain. Still, that doesn't make them among the best in the world. Some of the best producers are:

Balada	*Jean Leon*
René Barbier	*Parxet-Alella*
Marques de Monistrol	*Torres*

Sparkling Wines of Penedes

The major grapes are Xarello, Macabeo and Parellada. Called Espumoso (ess-poo-moe-so), most are made by the traditional methode champenoise and are thus entitled to use the word CAVA on the label—look for it. Attractive, dry, small bubble and pretty good values. The most popular producers are:

Castellblanch	*Lembey*
Cordorniu	*Paul Cheneau*
Freixenet	*Segura-Vuidas*

Summary

You're probably familiar with many of the Espumoso sparkling wine names. They're fairly palatable and reasonably priced if the seller hasn't called them "champagne" and boosted the price accordingly. However, I recommend California's methode champenoise sparklers first. The white wines of Spain are modest, you can do better. But many of the Rioja and Penedes reds are worthy. They're good and they're inexpensive, except when a store or restaurant, through avarice, decides the romance of a Spanish wine will support an unconscionable markup. There's some of that going around.

Sherry

Located in southern Spain in the region of Andalusia around the city of Jerez de la Frontera. Sherry is a fortified wine, meaning that after fermentation of the dry white wine, brandy is added, which raises the alcoholic content to around 17% to 19%. Aging pretty much determines quality. Sherry is a blend of vintages that are aged in barrels by a system called Solera. Barrels are stacked in rows one above the other, oldest wines on the bottom. As wine is drawn from the bottom row for bottling, it is replaced by the younger wine from the row above. Those from the second row are replaced by wine from the third row and so on. At each stage the younger wines refresh the older ones. What finally reaches the shelf in your market is probably a blend from several Soleras. Naturally, there are no vintage labeled sherries. The major grape is the Palomino with some use of Pedro Ximenez.

Types of Sherry

Fino (fee-no) One of the two basic types of Sherry. The other is Oloroso. The best are pale, light-bodied and completely dry. About 17% alcohol. Inexpensive to moderate. The less expensive are often just a bit sweet, not unpleasantly so at all.

Oloroso (o-lo-ro-so)—With Fino, the two basic types of Sherry. Intense, dark, full-bodied and higher in alcohol, up to 21%. Dry as they mature but many are sweetened with the Pedro Ximenez grape to become Cream Sherry. Inexpensive to moderate.

Manzanilla (mahn-thah-nee-yah)—A kind of Fino. The driest of all, very pale. About 17% alcohol. Small production. Inexpensive to moderate.

Amontillado (ah-mon-tee-yah-doe)—Actually an older Fino. More amber in color, naturally dry. Before shipping they are usually blended with some sweet wine to become slightly sweet. Nuttier and higher alcohol than Finos. Inexpensive to moderate.

Popular Houses

Look for these names, they are among the very best:

Barbadillo	*Duff Gordon*	*Emilio Lustau*
Luis Caballero	*Garvey*	*Osborne*
Croft	*Gonzalez Byass*	*Sandeman*
Pedro Domecq	*Harvey*	*Dry Sack**

*Dry Sack, under the firm of Williams and Humbert, is very popular. It is a medium sweet blend of Oloroso and Amontillado.

Sherry Summary

Sherries are wonderful wines for pre-prandial sipping. With or without friends they are great mood enhancers and appetite stimulators. The Finos, Manzanillas and Amontillados go well with appetizers, light dishes, soups, shellfish and nuts. Save the drier Olorosos for spicy dishes or pour them over ice cream for dessert. Serve Cream Sherry with fruit desserts and after dinner conversation. Serve all sherries chilled but never on the rocks. They may be recorked with impunity but the Finos should be consumed or tightly stoppered and refrigerated. Prices range from inexpensive to moderate and, with a little experimentation for not much money, you'll surely find a favorite.

I like Sherry, dry to sweet and everything in between. I think you probably haven't had one in a long time and will welcome this re-introduction.

TWO WINES OF
Portugal

Port

Port comes from the Duoro region in the northern part of Portugal. Portugal does make regular white, red and sparkling wines, but their glory lies with Port. Port is a fortified wine. Neutral wine spirits, high in alcohol, are added to the base wine, stopping fermentation and retaining some sugar. The result is a sweet wine containing up to 20% alcohol. Most Port exported to the U.S. is labeled as Porto in order to distinguish the real Portuguese Port from what we make here. Incidentally, some of ours aren't bad at all. The major grapes used are: *Tinta Roriz, Tinta Francisca* and *Tinta Cao.*

Two Types of Port

Wood Aged—These non-vintage Ports are aged in wood. When they are bottled, much of their heavy sediment is left behind, making them immediately drinkable. There are two categories of wood aged Port.

> *Ruby Port*—Deep colored and sweet with up-front fruit flavors. Aged in wood up to three or four years. Ready to drink. Least expensive.

> *Tawny Port*—A ruby grown older. A blend of vintages that has been aged up to ten or twenty years or more. The wine has developed a more amber color and is mellower. Ready to drink. Inexpensive to expensive.

Vintage Port—Made from the best grapes blended from the best vineyards and from a single harvest. The year will be on the bottle. Not every year is declared a "vintage year"—only about three out of ten. They are bottled after two years in wood, leaving proper maturity up to the patience of the buyer. Most require at least ten years bottle aging and will improve for 50 years or more. (Frankly, I don't have much incentive for stocking up on the latest declared vintage, 1991.) Expensive in their youth, becoming more so as they mature. Serious Port lovers try to stock up when the vintage is first released. However, there are ways around this Vintage Port price thing. I experiment, with great satisfaction, among Ports labeled Late Bottled Vintage (LBV) or Vintage Character. They are made from the best grapes of non-declared years but are aged longer before bottling. Most of their sediment is left behind and they are drinkable now at a much lower price.

Some of the best Port producers are listed below. Look for these famous names:

Cockburn	Graham	Smith-Woodhouse
Croft	Robertson	Taylor Fladgate
Dow	Sandeman	Warre

Note that all of these Port houses have English names. Traditional lovers of Port, the British established these great houses; some are hundreds of years old.

Summary

Port has had its ups and downs but it's in a modest revival stage now as prices have dropped. The better and best are expensive but there are many, readily available, that can provide great enjoyment at a modest price.

A small glass of Port after dinner is a wonderful way to linger at table. If the company is agreeable it delays departure, continues the sparkling conversation and adds just the right note of hedonistic pleasure. Not too much now, you do want those good people to arrive home safely.

Madeira

An island in the Atlantic, off the coast of Morocco. The Portuguese island of Madeira became famous for its wines during our American colonial days. It was a favorite of Americans and the British. It is produced in a very unusual way. Made from four grape varieties, the basic wine is fortified with neutral spirits to increase alcohol levels to 18%-20%. The sweeter varieties are fortified to the desired sweetness during fermentation, other varieties are fermented dry and then fortified. The new wine is then transferred to tanks containing heating coils, or into casks that are then placed in heated rooms, and literally baked for several months. As you might expect, the wines develop a burnt flavor. After the bake job, the wine goes into casks for further aging—a minimum of three years up to 20 years or more.

Five Types of Madeira

Most Madeiras are labeled with the grape name and they each have their own style and degree of sweetness.

Sercial—The driest. Pale and light. You'd drink it before a meal.

Verdelho—Slightly sweet and fuller than Sercial. Again, before a meal or with pastries.

Bual—Soft and rich, sweeter than the two above. After dinner sipping or as a dessert wine.

Malmsey—The sweetest of all. Dark, rich and full bodied. Alone after dinner as you reflect upon the riches before you.

Rainwater—A generic name, not a grape. Popular, made in a pale, slightly sweet style.

If your wine merchant carries some Madeiras you won't be overwhelmed with the selection. They're not the most sought after wines. Some shippers to reassure you are:

Barbeito	*Cossart Gordon*	*Rutherford & Miles*
Blandy	*Madeira Wine Co.*	*Shortridge Lawson*

Summary

Now, I don't expect you to go right out and buy a bottle of Madeira. They're certainly not high on my list of must-haves. But if you are curious, you may find it a very pleasant change. Nothing tastes quite like the earthy, nutty, toastiness of a Madeira. They increase in price as their age increases. A five-year-old Malmsey is affordable. A ten-year-old is very expensive and they positively rocket as they reach over 100 years of age.

I hope including Madeira hasn't wasted your time. I could have left it out, but the making of the wine is such a unique process and the very word has such a mystique about it that I thought you might be interested.

THE WINES OF
Other Countries

Australia

Once in a while someone asks me about Australian wines—why is everyone talking about them? Are they any good? The answer to the second question is yes, and that's why everyone is talking about them. That and the fact that they are excellent values. The Aussies set out to crack this market a few years ago, and they did.

They make wines from most of the grape varieties we use and, like us, they label their wines with the name of the grape. A wine labeled with a varietal name must contain at least 85% of the grape. If blended, which many of their better wines are, both grapes must be named in order of quantity. It's easy to shop for Australian wines.

White Wines

White wine grapes make up over 60% of vineyard acreage. Chardonnay, Riesling, Sauvignon Blanc, Semillon and Muscat are the major grapes and make the best wine. Especially Semillon and blends of Semillon and Chardonnay or Sauvignon Blanc. Their sweet Muscats are good, too.

Red Wines

Cabernet Sauvignon, Pinot Noir and Merlot are grown, but Shiraz is the most widely planted grape and makes the best red wine. In the U.S. and France the grape is called Syrah. Blends of Cabernet Sauvignon and Shiraz make lovely wines, but the greatest Australian wine is Penfold's Grange Hermitage. Made from 100% Shiraz, it is sought after and expensive. One of the hottest wines around is Rosemount's Shiraz. It is soft, rich and full of berry flavors. For under $8, it's a must-try.

Australian wines are widely distributed in the U.S. and so far they've kept prices very competitive. In selecting, be guided by names of some of the best producers:

Brown Bros	Montrose	Rosemount
Lindemans	Mountadam	Seppelt
Hardy	Orlando	Mark Swann
Miramar	Petaluma	Wolf Blass
Mildara	Penfolds	Yalumba

New Zealand

Much has been written about the wonderful wine being produced in New Zealand. During a recent trip I tasted a wide range of wines in order to get a feel for the product. Spotty availability makes that difficult to do in the U.S. My general impression was that there are many good whites but a dearth of acceptable reds.

White Wines

The most common white wine is made from the Muller Thurgau grape. Tending to sweetness, some are light and fruity, some just plain blah. We had some excellent Chardonnays and some very good Sauvignon Blancs. In fact, one Chardonnay was memorable from the Kumeu River Winery.

Red Wines

Cabernet Sauvignon, Merlot and Pinot Noir are the major grapes. The best red wine we encountered was an '87 Vidal's Hawkes Bay Reserve Cabernet Sauvignon (85%) and Merlot (15%).

Other good wineries making both white and red wines are—Montana (largest), Corbans, Coopers Creek, Villa Maria, Selaks, Matua Valley, Stoneleigh, Cloudy Bay and Nobilo.

Kiwi Fruit Wine

I'm not making this up, there really is wine made from the Kiwi fruit. South of Auckland, outside the neat little city of Tauranga, is the Preston Kiwi Fruit Winery. We entered by a narrow dirt road through trellised vineyards to the small tasting room. There we tasted their full line of wines and were amazed at their similarity to grape wine. There is some natural sugar to support fermentation, but I assume some chaptalization (adding sugar) is necessary to reach an acceptable level of alcohol. There was a "Medium" which is somewhat sweet, a "Dry" which would be suitable as a food wine and a "Premium" which is dry, oak aged and had some of the characteristics of a Sauvignon Blanc. We also tasted their bulk processed sparkling wine which, though sweet, was more agreeable than some of California's 2 for $5 sparklers.

To make a judgement on a country's wines by visiting tasting rooms and imbibing from restaurant wine lists during a two week journey is somewhat subjective, if not presumptuous. But it's the best I could do, considering the scarcity of New Zealand wines in the US. I'd have done better in Great Britain or Japan, who do import more of them. So, why did I bring it up? One, because they're coming on; two, in case you wondered; and three, because I wanted to tell you about Kiwi Fruit Wine.

Argentina

Moving into South America, Argentina is deserving of some notice. First of all, they drink a lot of wine, most of what they produce. In other words, they enjoy their own product and they make a lot of it, more than any other South American country. And second, they make very good red wines.

White Wines

Their white wines are not considered outstanding, but they are working on increasing the quality of Chardonnay, Sauvignon Blanc, Semillon and Chenin Blanc. I expect they'll succeed.

Red Wines

A different story from the white, here they already succeed. Many of their wineries are making excellent Cabernet Sauvignon and Malbec. Other grapes used are Merlot, Pinot Noir and Sangiovese.

Argentina is not a big exporter of wine. Finding them in the U.S. is not an easy task. The following list contains good wineries that do export to the U.S.

Bianchi	Navarro-Correas	Penaflor
Canale	José Orfila	San Telmo
Humberto	Etchart	Weinert

Bodegas Esmeralda for Catena and Trumpeter wines

Chile

Several years ago a new restaurant opened in my vicinity. So, as is my wont, I chose a noon hour when I had been abandoned and gave it a try. Of course my eye went first to their house wine offering. And this was my introduction to Chilean wines. The house white was a Concha y Toro Sauvignon Blanc blended with Semillon. The house red was a Concha y Toro Cabernet Sauvignon blended with Merlot. Both knocked my socks off at $2 a glass.

In Chile, the best white wines are Sauvignon Blanc and

Semillon. Chardonnay and Riesling are showing promise. The best red wine, perhaps the best in South America, is Cabernet Sauvignon. Malbec, Merlot and some Pinot Noir are also grown.

After my introduction to Chilean wines, I went out of my way to take advantage of the values. But alas, things seem to be slipping—prices are still low but the quality I enjoyed is not being maintained. Perhaps I expect too much. Nevertheless, there are still good wines for a small price and I recommend you give them a try. By all means look for the Concha y Toro wines which are maintaining quality. Other wineries are:

Canepa	Vina Del Mar	San Pedro
Carmen	Mitjans	Santa Rita
Cousino-Macul	Montes	Undurrago

Some Others

I'll make brief mention of a few other countries that have a special wine or wines to distinguish them. You would have trouble finding them here, but you certainly want to know about them if you go there.

Austria—A wine drinking country. In fact, what they produce they pretty much drink up. Little chance of finding them here. Most of their wine is white, hearty and good; or insipid rosés. The whites follow the German line of varieties such as Riesling and Muller-Thurgau. Reds? Don't even think about it.

Greece—Many years ago I had horrible wines in Greece. My, how I suffered in the process of experimenting. But, today I understand there is great improvement. I did like their Retsina, although some people describe the taste as akin to battery acid. (I really wouldn't know.) You might like its pine-resin flavor. Look for red and white wines from Achaia-Clauss, Boutari, Andrew Cambas and Carras. If you can't find them, the best way to try Greek wines in the U.S. is in a Greek restaurant. The wines go with the food.

Hungary—Making good wine from some very old vineyards. And their greatest, a sweet wine made in varying degrees of sweetness, called Tokay (Tokaji). They are very expensive. I tasted one once, and it was a memorable experience. Their reds are led in fame by the full bodied, Bull's Blood (Bikaver). Both available here with a search.

Israel—As you might expect, the area has been producing wine for centuries. But until several years ago the emphasis was mainly on sweet Kosher wines. Now progress is being made with new plantings of French Colombard, Sauvignon Blanc and Chardonnay and such red varieties as Cabernet Sauvignon and Petite Sirah. These wines are labeled either with proprietary names or the grape variety. Wines from Carmel and Yarden are available in the U.S.

South Africa—Early settlers made wine of an indifferent sort but over the years all of that has changed, as has their reputation. Chenin Blanc is the leading white grape. Chardonnay, Sauvignon Blanc and Riesling are becoming more important. The finest red wine is Cabernet Sauvignon. Merlot, Shiraz and Pinot Noir are also grown. Pinotage, a cross between Pinot Noir and Cinsault, makes a good and popular wine. Availability of South African wines is meager, but the product is good and they'll make their way here eventually.

WINE

Intelligence

It is popular today among wine people to scoff at some of the traditions and rituals that go along with serving and drinking wine. Sort of proves what nice, down-to-earth human beings they are. A common attitude is, "wine is to be enjoyed, cut out all the nonsense, just do your own thing." I agree, to some extent. There are those pretentious snobs who overdo the niceties of wine imbibing, and they are a pain. But, like it or not, wine does have traditions of social significance. And just as the rules of etiquette are guides to acceptable social behavior in our society, so are some of the rituals involving wine. More to the point, they usually make sense.

The pages that follow provide helpful information for those interested in the procedures and ways of wine enjoyment. But with this difference—we'll try to loosen up some of the hard and fast rules of selecting, storing, ordering, serving and so on. Or at least explain the why of them. You will notice that interspersed here and there are some imperative opinions of my own—which should be taken very much to heart in that they represent the real truth.

Through it all, remember this—wine is to be enjoyed, and whatever you enjoy is right. Just make sure that you use a large enough glass.

Where To Buy Wine

You're having company for dinner. You've gone to a great deal of trouble in procuring the makings for a special meal. But at the last moment you remember—the wine! You dash to the nearest liquor store, ask what's good with steak and walk out with an overpriced, long-on-the-shelf bottle of Beaujolais. Now, why on earth would anyone give less thought to the wine than to the dinner? They deserve equal consideration.

In the above scenario. the answer to where to buy wine is—
at the same market where you shop regularly. They may not
have the very best prices on wine but in the total mix of pro-
ducts purchased, you will average out okay. There are some
supermarkets that do a superb job in marketing wines. They
have good buyers, good selection and reasonable prices. However, be aware that some stores in a chain, depending on location
and customer profile, concentrate on wine more than others.

If one resorts to the nearest liquor store, odds are against
doing well. Their emphasis may be on beer, pints, snacks,
lottery tickets and other volume items. Except for specials,
wine is not the focus of their merchandising effort. Certainly,
there are exceptions. Some liquor stores take pride in carrying
a good selection of wines at fair prices, though seldom the
lowest. You will have to search and compare to find the exceptions. Convenience is a factor.

Drug store chains are generally the worst places to buy wine.
The highest prices of all, a selection of only the most popular
varietals, heavy on jug wines and no informed help. It is beyond
me why any otherwise careful shopper would buy wine in a
drug store, except to take advantage of specials or because they
are already there to buy aspirin.

The best place to buy wine is at the specialty wine shops, the
merchants who sell nothing but wine, at a discount and in
volume. You get selection, continuity, usually the lowest price
and knowledgeable guidance in the right environment.

If you are willing to give up selection, continuity (finding your
favorite wine on each trip) and help, then the discount clubs or
warehouse stores are next best. You could drive a few miles out
of your way and save enough to buy an extra bottle or two.

Wine Bottle Sizes

Since 1979 federal regulations require that all American and imported wines sold in the United States must use metric-system sized bottles. The net contents of the bottle must be shown on the label or impressed on the glass.

Bottles	Metric Capacity	U.S. Ounces
¼ bottle (split)	187 ml	6.3
½ bottle	375 ml	12.7
Reg. bottle	750 ml	25.4
Oversize	1.0 liter	33.8
Magnum	1.5 liters	50.7 (2 750 ml bottles)
Double Magnum	3.0 liters	101.4 (4 750 ml bottles)
Jeroboam	4.5 liters	152.1 (6 750 ml bottles)
Imperial	6.0 liters	202.8 (8 750 ml bottles)

Not enough half bottles are offered in stores or on wine lists. They are a nice size for one person, modest consuming couples or to solve the, I'm having fish, you're having steak problem. The quarter bottle, which is a split, is a one glass serving. Both half and quarter bottles, when available, are usually overpriced. I suppose they are a bother for the seller who would rather stick to inventorying one bottle size and get a higher ticket sale. There are a few restaurants that go out of their way to provide a selection of half bottles and they hold a warm spot in my heart.

A new wine bottle size of 500 milliliters was recently introduced, but so far without much success. It is a better size for two people than the 375 ml half bottle. Let's hope eventually it becomes more available.

How To Store Wine

One time I saw wine stored atop a refrigerator in a small family owned restaurant. Few places could be worse. The top of a refrigerator provides the three major elements that are the enemies of proper wine storage—light, heat and vibration. Avoid these and you'll have a reasonable place to store wine.

What is the point of storing wine? So it is available for any occasion, planned or not. So it has had time to settle down, traveling from a store can temporarily upset a good red wine. And to save money, you could buy a fine bottle upon release from the winery that after a few years might be too costly. However, we'll assume few of us purchase wine in the hope that it will appreciate from $6 to $120 a bottle 20 years later. I got lucky. Just store wine so it is well rested and available when you want it.

Assuming you do not have a cool cellar (if you do, I'm envious), nor a temperature controlled wine storage area in your home, I suggest first of all a cabinet and second a closet. Consider this about both areas—they are a box within a box (a closed area within your house). Wine bottles gradually take on the temperature surrounding them and tend to stabilize each other— they provide their own temperature control. So, there is really less fluctuation in the temperature of wines reasonably stored than is supposed. For years I have maintained storage for from 200 to 300 bottles in a closet in my home. And have even moved prized bottles 2000 miles from one closet to another. I have successfully stored good bottles of wine in that environment for over 20 years. There have been some disappointments, but those were my fault. I misjudged the staying power of the wine. Of course, some wines are not meant to age, you do have to stay on top of the situation.

If it's a case or two of wine that you keep on hand, leave the bottles in the case (added insulation) and store the case in a cabinet or closet. If you decide to go my route, clear out a closet, with your spouse's permission of course, and either build, have built, or buy suitable shelves or racks for storage. Then start filling the racks. All bottles should be stored on their sides so the corks are kept moist, protecting the wine against air.

If all of this is a bother or you don't have the space, let your wine merchant store the wine. Many have temperature controlled "lockers" and will store the case lot wines you buy from them at a modest annual fee. It is possible the fee could be less than the increasing value of the well stored wine, although I wouldn't depend on it.

One important caveat. If high temperatures are maintained or there are radical temperature swings, all of my confident assertions are out the window. If you let the temperature drop to 45⁰ in the winter and increase to 85⁰ in the summer, your wine will be at risk. Remember that heat accelerates aging and wide fluctuations in temperature are harmful. Modest and gradual fluctuations between 60⁰ and 75⁰ should be no cause for concern.

When Wine Is Ready

This section properly follows How To Store Wine; they are related. Most white wines, rosés, light reds and sparkling wines are ready to drink when you buy them. Storing them for long periods of time under any conditions is risky. One time I decided to assemble different years of a favorite Chardonnay in order to conduct a vertical tasting. I had an '84, '85 and '86 in my "cellar." I purchased an '87 and an '88 in 1990. The '84 was almost gone, the '85 showed signs of deterioration and the '86 was flirting with a late life crisis. Granted, there are some

Chardonnays that would have stood the test of this span of time. However, this wine, which is lovely in its youth, was not made to age. Many are not, so why risk it?

It is more difficult to advise on red wines. I suggested that light reds should be drunk young, don't hold them for more than two or three years. But how do you know which reds are light? Well, you just have to try, ask or guess. If it tastes light, it is. If it tastes good to you, even young, go ahead and drink it. Some typical light reds are Gamay, the French Beaujolais and the Italian Bardolino, Valpolicella and lesser Chiantis. California Pinot Noir and the French Burgundies will tolerate more bottle aging, but often are quite drinkable when you buy them. The Spanish Riojas are made to drink young but they'll age a few years properly stored. The greatest red wine for longevity is Cabernet Sauvignon, in France the Bordeaux wines. The great Italian Barolo, Barberesco, Barbera and Brunello age well, as do the California Merlot, Syrah and Zinfandel. Make sure to check the vintage year on these wines; they shouldn't be born yesterday.

Of course there are exceptions, cheaply made wine from inferior grapes may not age to the norm. Wines are like people, if they are from sturdy stock and well cared for, they will live longer. When in doubt, ask. A good wine merchant will know and will tell you straight.

Opening the Bottle and Corkscrews

I always open a bottle with great anticipation, and a corkscrew. How do you open a bottle? Well, you could use one of those dreadful spirals with a wooden handle on the end, I see them in otherwise well-utensiled kitchens. Or as a last resort you could hammer the cork into the bottle. There are better ways.

Opening Still Wines

Cut the top capsule below the second lip of the bottle and remove. Wipe off any collected gunk, remove the cork and wipe the bottle neck inside and out.

There are several types of corkscrews, but the one I like best is called the Waiter's Friend. It fits in pocket or purse like a jackknife so you are always prepared for a bottle opening emergency. The spiral, or worm, is turned into the cork all the way, a claw is positioned on the lip of the bottle and the cork is levered out quickly and easily. I think it is the best because it is portable, fast, sure and inexpensive. Sommeliers and waiters use it and I proved it in a "cork out" with a bartender friend. He used an Ah-So, the two-pronged doo-hickey that slips down the sides of the cork (sometimes it works, sometimes it doesn't). I beat him by a yank; he had an easy cork. Challenged again, he used the familiar Wing-Lever type where, as you screw into the cork, the levers rise on each side and you push down on them to extract the cork. It is solid and sure, but slow. I was sipping a glass of wine by the time he finished. If you've counted, you'll realize there were now four opened bottles. We had a nice afternoon.

A relative newcomer is the Screwpull—it's a sure-fire cork retriever, but requires more fiddling around. The length of the worm is its biggest advantage, it is long enough to extract the longest cork. In buying a corkscrew, consider the length of the worm, it should be no less than 2 inches long and 2½ inches is better.

Opening Sparkling Wines

Never try to open a Champagne or sparkling wine bottle with a corkscrew. It is dangerous, there's a lot of pressure in there. First remove the foil covering the cork, then holding your left palm protectively over the cork, untwist the wire. I leave the loosened wire on the cork for a better grip. Holding the wired cork firmly in the left hand, tilt the bottle away from yourself and others and slowly twist and pull the bottle from the bottom with your right hand. The cork should be eased out with a soft pop or sigh, leaving the contents in the bottle, wasting no wine and endangering no bystanders. Leave the foaming, spurting, sparkling wine bouts to the World Series winners. They can afford it.

Breathing and Decanting

Breathing

Lots of controversy here. Does a wine need to breathe? Well, yes, many red wines benefit by exposure to air. But consider this, an opened bottle has an exposed surface about the size of a nickel. Your meal would be over by the time any real aeration took place. So, I usually tell the waiter or wine steward to allow me my obligatory swirl-sniff-and-taste, then pour our glasses to about half way and let it breathe while we eat our salad. Decanting is also a good way to aerate a wine, but if it isn't necessary for other reasons, my way is a good way.

Many red wines don't require a breathing period, they just aren't that complex. Cabernets, Merlot, Pinot Noir and Zinfandel often benefit. The words for these wines, when first opened, might include: tight, closed in, inaccessible. It is truly amazing how a wine can open up, taking on a whole new character and richness as it breathes. How do you know when? In a restaurant they'll usually suggest opening the bottle for breathing time. If they do not, ask if it might not be a good idea, or have them pour it. At home just open the bottle an hour or two before serving or, if you forget, pour it as soon as possible before consuming. You'll work it out.

One other thing, some very grand old red Bordeaux and Burgundies could be fragile and fall apart in a few minutes if allowed much air. You may never be confronted with this problem.

Decanting

There are occasions for decanting, but they are rare. Not long ago, in a nice restaurant, the captain brought decanter and candle to our table along with a five-year-old bottle of Cabernet Sauvignon. In my view, he just wanted to put on a show. I asked if he thought the wine were old enough to have much sediment and he admitted, probably not. So we decided to dispense with the procedure.

Older red wines, eight to ten years or more, often develop sediment. It is not a defect, it is a good thing. It is the by-product of aging as the wine throws off tannins and red skin pigments. In the process, wines that, when younger, may have been astringent and puckery, become softer and much more agreeable.

If the bottle has been handled carefully, the sediment should be resting along the side of the bottle, or at the bottom if allowed to stand for a time. I was horrified one time in France as the captain came up from the cellar gaily swinging my bottle of Chateau Haut-Brion. It was thoroughly roiled with sediment and quite undrinkable. When I complained to madam-owner, she said, "but of course, it is a very old wine." But when she saw the result, it was whisked away and replaced.

If a bottle appears to contain sediment, handle and pour it carefully to avoid roiling. You can usually pour the wine out and over any sediment. If it is a very old wine and obviously contains a large amount of sediment, you should decant it. Pour slowly into a decanter with a light behind the bottle so you can see what's going on inside. A candle is not necessary, but usually most practical, any bright light will do. Stop when you reach the point where you see that sediment is about to enter the decanter. Give what's left in the bottle time to settle; sometimes you'll reap a bit more clear wine. On the other hand, a little bit of gook settling into the bottom of your glass won't hurt; you paid for it.

So, sediment isn't a bad thing. Nor are crystals, sometimes found in wine or on the bottom of a cork. Tartaric acid is a natural acid in wine, as the wine ages it throws off cream of tartar crystals, which are most evident in white wines. It is natural, harmless and tasteless and no reason to send a bottle back.

The Right Glass

Wineglasses should be big so they provide a decent portion of wine without being filled, so you can tilt and observe the color, so the wine can be swirled without slopping it on the tablecloth and so you can stick your nose in it and enjoy the bouquet. It's okay to drink out of it, too. I have been at dinner parties where the hosts spent much time trying to keep their treasured, thimble-sized, crystal glasses filled. They may be pretty (the glasses) but they're best suited for an aperitif.

ALL-PURPOSE   FLUTE

There are wineglasses sized and shaped specifically for almost every type of wine. Fortunately, you really need only one all-purpose glass for all white and red still table wines. It should be sizeable, twelve ounces is good. Ten ounces should be the minimum. The bowl should curve slightly inward at the top so the bouquet of the wine is concentrated. It should be clear, no tints, no color, and it should be plain surfaced, no etching or pattern. You want to see the wine. And finally, it must have a stem so the glass can be held without warming the bowl with your hand. A glass fulfilling all of these requirements is easy to find and can be had for as little as $1.50, or a Baccarat for $100 or more, or almost any price in between.

For sparkling wine and Champagne you will need a flute or tulip shaped glass (a flute is shown). If you have some of those old saucer shaped champagne glasses either donate them to Goodwill or drink a final toast and throw them into the fireplace. They are out of style, awkward to hold and dissipate the bubbles. Small flutes or tulips can be had in a neat six ounce size but an eight ounce will serve you better.

It is important that wineglasses be thoroughly rinsed after washing. The slightest soap residue can throw off a wine and in a sparkling wineglass can create a frenzy of overflowing foam.

Temperature, Serving and Recorking

Temperature

The temperature of your wine is so important. Most white wines are served too cold, which dulls the flavor. Most red wines are served too warm; they may taste flat and lifeless. White wines should be served at about 45°-55°. Red wines at so-called room temperature, about 60°-70°. So how do you know?

Why, you use my "20-20 method"—remove white wines from the refrigerator 20 minutes before serving and put red wines into the refrigerator 20 minutes before serving. Simple red wines like Beaujolais, Bardolino, Valpolicella and the jugs should be served slightly chilled. Champagne, sparkling wines and rosés are best served cold, just as they come from the refrigerator or chill them in an ice bucket about half filled with ice cubes and water. Do not put wine in the freezer compartment. Do not put ice cubes in white wine. Do not put reds in hot water if they're too cold. Wine should adjust slowly. Be merciful.

How Many Pours?

There are 25.4 ounces in a regular 750 milliliter bottle. Remembering to pour a glass less than halfway, a bottle will give you about six pours using 10 ounce glasses and about five pours using 12 ounce glasses. Actually, four ounces of wine is a decent amount in any size glass. It's an attitude, don't look at it as being a small amount of wine, think of it as being a large glass.

Serving

All wine glasses go to the upper right of the place setting. If you serve more than one wine, a fresh glass should be provided. If you have glasses of different sizes, use the smaller for white wine and the larger for red.

If you are serving more than one wine to your lucky guests, serve dry whites before red, light wines before heavier wines, young wines before older wines and dry wines before sweet. But that's just common sense, you knew it already.

Pour glasses no more than half full. Giving a slight twist as you raise the bottle after pouring will prevent dripping on the tablecloth. Don't cover the bottle with a towel, the label should be visible to interested guests. It is correct for the host* to

*I consider unnecessary the use of *ess* on the end of words to denote the feminine gender. A host is a host and I eschew the word hostess just as I do all associated *ess* ending words. Since I have your attention I could not resist making this point. Call me a feminist if you will, or better yet a wordist...*ists* are okay.

pour a small amount to taste and approve and then pour for the guests. It is all right for the guests to ask for more if it is obvious there is more (my rule).

Dinner Party Gift Wine

Let's say you've planned dinner with the appropriate wine and a guest brings a bottle as a gift. Do they expect you to serve it? They should not. You can express your appreciation by saying that it will go beautifully with a future dinner. Of course, there are exceptions, especially among wine loving friends. With your prior knowledge, they may bring a wine that will pair interestingly with the one you've selected. It can be great fun, especially if it's a bottle of Chateau Leoville Las Cases.

When I arrive at a dinner party with bottle in hand, I make it clear to the hosts that it is for their future enjoyment.

Recorking

White wine not consumed can be stored for two or three days in the refrigerator, jug wines with a screw cap, longer. If the cork is swollen and difficult to replace, clean the top and reverse it. The same for red wine but more than a day in the fridge is risky, best to consume it. There are many devices for stoppering opened wine bottles, but cork seems to be the best. The clasp type closure for sparkling wine bottles works very well and properly seated and secured will hold the wine in the refrigerator for several days. Some people leave the sparkling wine bottle open and insert a teaspoon, handle first into the bottle. It seems to work; I can't imagine why.

Tasting Wine

Evaluating a wine takes some thought. There are wine drinkers who don't really taste the wine and there are those who thoughtfully do both, drink and taste.

Here are suggestions to help you in evaluating wine at organized tastings, individually at your own table, or others, and in a restaurant. If you do it subtly in the last three locations, no one will think you've gone over the edge.

Using the three senses of sight, smell and taste, follow this pattern:

Sight

Hold a less than half full glass by the stem, raise it toward the light and tip it away from you. Note color, both hue and density. Note clarity, the wine should be clear and brilliant. It should look pretty.

Smell

Swirl wine in the glass to release the odors. Sniff for aroma, which is the fragrance of the grape, and bouquet, the more subtle fragrance that comes from fermenting and aging. The wine should smell good.

Taste

Sip the wine, hold it in your mouth, roll it around with your tongue. Think about what you taste—tartness or smoothness, degree of dryness or sweetness, richness, body and balance, are all elements in harmony? And then the finish (lingering flavors), the longer the good flavors stay on your palate, the better the wine. Finally, your overall impression of the flavor and quality of the wine. The wine should taste good.

Your evaluation of the wine needn't be anything technical or profound. But this procedure will get your mind in the right place and increase your enjoyment of the wine, the meal and the entire experience.

Restaurant Ordering

No one should be intimidated by the process of ordering wine in a restaurant anywhere at any time. If you know enough about wine to go through the list and come up with a wine you like, that will go with the food you've ordered and at a price you are willing to pay, you have no problem. If you are just a bit doubtful about what to select, or even have no idea at all where to start, the waiter, captain or manager will be more than pleased to assist you, and you have no problem.

The wine list should be presented to you with the menu. If it is not, ask for it right away so you may plan the meal and move right on to selecting the wine or vice versa.

Different Food, Different Wine

If different dishes are ordered, a bottle of sparkling wine or a rosé might be just the thing. However, if you would rather have a white wine to go with the fish and a red wine to go with the lamb, look for half-bottle sizes on the list. Unfortunately, not many restaurants list a wide selection. In that case you could inquire as to the house wine or those wines that are served by the glass. Not long ago the house wine in many otherwise good restaurants was a less than adequate jug wine. That is not so much the case today. Most good restaurants provide a selection of popular varietal wines by the glass. I know of one seafood-steak-and-chops type of restaurant that has 10 wines by the glass plus specials of the week. Now that is the right thing to do! Nevertheless, if there are four or more people in your party, it will be cost effective to order a bottle or two, perhaps one white and one red. Your waiter will likely mention this.

Prices

Of course price is an important factor for anyone not on an expense account and even then it ought to be. The general rule for prices on a wine list is, two times the retail price, which really means, the suggested retail price. A $10 bottle of wine in a discount wine shop may be $14 in a supermarket and $28 or more on a wine list. It is a loose rule, some restaurants are under, some are over. It is almost impossible to give good information about wine list pricing (except to say that overall some lists are expensive, some moderate and some inexpensive); it is too variable and sometimes irrational. There is one guide I am concerned with—a wine list should include wines at prices that are compatible with the restaurant's menu prices. If entrees average $14 there should be some wines priced in that area, at least a few under $20. Well balanced wine lists will include a selection of well known wines at reasonable prices as a basis for the overall list.

If, in the process of ordering wine with guests at the table, you don't want to discuss price with the waiter, simply point to a price on the list and ask if a wine in that category would be suitable. He or she will understand and be helpful in that price area. If they don't, you've got a dummy and you will just have to bull your way through.

Restaurants with in-depth wine lists provide an opportunity to try rare or hard to find wines. But be aware that you will pay dearly. If the bottle is available at retail I would rather consume it at home and save at least half of the restaurant price. Also, a really fine bottle may be better analyzed and appreciated in the home where there is less noise and distraction...well, maybe.

Serving

If you ordered the wine, the waiter should present the un-opened bottle to you to assure it is the correct wine. Be sure to examine the bottle. Many times I have been presented with the wrong bottle, sometimes it was a misunderstanding or a mistake, or it was because they were out of the wine ordered and hoped the substitute would get by. Sometimes the substitute is acceptable and higher priced. If they do not volunteer to charge the lower price of the bottle first ordered, suggest that it might be appropriate. After all, it was their substitution.

Once your approval is obtained, the waiter will remove the cork and place it on the table, ostensibly for you to smell. I suggest you check to see if the name on the cork agrees with the label, then feel the end to determine if it is damp and has done its job. To me, smelling the cork is kind of silly. Smelling and tasting the wine is what gets the job done. The waiter will then pour a small amount into your glass. Take your time, make sure the wine smells and tastes right. If so, nod and the waiter will pour others at the table (correctly, no more than half a glass) before returning to your glass. If the wine has any "off" odors, and by that I mean it just doesn't smell right, give it a chance, taste it. Sometimes the pouring process releases an unpleasant odor and that's the end of it. That first whiff may be misleading. If the wine tastes bad, you have every right to quietly inform the waiter. You may ask that the wine be tasted to verify or you may simply state that the wine is bad and ask to have it replaced. I have seldom had to do this but when I have, there has never been an argument. It is a different matter if the wine is sound and you just don't like it.

Finally, a good restaurant is one that cares about its customers. That caring is reflected not only in the ambience and the food, but in the wine list and the wine service. At no time should any of these elements be cause for discomfort. All things should be in balance to provide you with a pleasant dining experience. But I add this—a pleasant dining experience is a partnership with the restaurant, you have a responsibility, too. To honor a reservation on time, to cancel if it cannot be fulfilled, and to understand the kitchen cannot accommodate everyone at precisely 7 o'clock and you may have to take a later table. That's about it, you've done your part, now the success of the evening is up to the restaurant staff. Bon appetit.

Wine and Food Pairings

What wine goes with what food is subjective, there are few hard and fast rules. The old, white wine with fish and chicken and red wine with meat is basic and makes sense. However, if your taste goes in another direction, that's fine. There are people who don't care for red wine (or it gives them a headache) and drink white wine with all kinds of food.

In the section on Serving I mentioned that if you serve more than one wine it is best to serve white before red, light before heavier wines and dry before sweet. These rules are sensible in that they follow the natural order of foods served. But they are not mandatory. Today, a light red wine with some fish and chicken dishes is quite acceptable.

I could take up a couple of pages with charts listing the ideal pairing of certain foods with certain wines. I think it is much better that you follow your own good taste sense. You just know a delicate fish would not sit well accompanied by a hearty Petite Sirah. So, think about the "weight" of the food and the intensity of any sauces that may be added and choose a compatible wine.

If the food is simple, light fish or chicken, a simple white wine is called for. Some prefer a contrast, a more complex wine with a simple dish. Heavier flavored fish such as tuna and salmon will do well with white wine or light-bodied reds. With ham, a rosé, off-dry white or light red. Veal, roast chicken, turkey or duck will support somewhat richer, heavier whites and reds. Beefsteak, roasts, game and pastas with meat sauce call for sturdy red wines. If you prefer white wine with these dishes, go right ahead, but we'll all feel sorry for you.

Putting wine with dessert is more difficult, sweet with sweet just doesn't work for me. But an Extra Dry Champagne or sparkling wine is wonderful with a sweet dessert. I prefer sweet dessert wines as a finish to a meal, after dessert or instead of. If there is cheese after the meal (or before) you have a decision to make. Some feel no red wine goes well with cheese (too fatty) but for my taste, that's too sweeping a restriction—what's better than Stilton with Port? Be guided by this, if the cheese is very strong it will kill the flavor of the wine, better to do without. Following are suggestions (gleaned from many sources, none of which agree entirely) for pairing some of the more popular cheeses with wine.

Brie and **Camembert**—Dry whites, sparkling wine, Cabernet, Merlot and Pinot Noir. If the cheese is overripe, forget the wine or experiment with a sweet wine.

Cheddar—Sauvignon Blanc, Pinot Noir, Dry Sherry, Port.

Gorganzola—Full reds, Merlot, Pinot Noir, Zinfandel.

Gouda—Most dry white wines. Dry Sherry.

Gruyere and **Swiss**—Chardonnay, off-dry Riesling, maybe Pinot Noir.

Jack—Chenin Blanc, Riesling, Pinot Noir, Gamay.

Port Salut—Sauvignon Blanc, Riesling, young reds.

Roquefort—Sweet whites like California Late Harvest wines and Muscat. Zinfandel and rich sherries.

Stilton—Muscat, Port, mature Cabernet Sauvignon, Zinfandel.

There are some foods that simply don't go with wine. Salads with vinegar based dressings, anchovies, strong cheese, eggs, except for omelets, which I like with a dry or off-dry white wine, citrus fruit and, I challenge you to find a wine that goes well with dill pickles and ice cream.

Pronunciation

I've heard people say, "oh, I'd get more into wine if I didn't have so much trouble with pronunciation." I know, I know, it's a problem for everyone at one time or another. I have heard sommeliers and maitre d's mispronounce wine names—like Montrachet, often mispronounced with the "t" (see below). No one is perfect but you won't get better if you don't try. No one will harm your parents if you mess up, honest.

Following are wine words you'll run across on wine lists, wine labels and in wine reading and discussion. I have omitted those you're likely to know or will seldom run across.

Aloxe Corton (ah-loks cor-tawn)
Alsace (al-zass)
Amontillado (ah-mon-tee-yah-doe)
Auslese (ouse-lay-zeh)
Ausone (oh-zon)
Barbaresco (bar-bah-ress-co)
Barbera (bar-bear-ah)
Bardolino (bar-doh-lee-no)
Barolo (bah-roh-lo)
Beaujolais (bo-jo-lay)
Botrytis Cinerea (bo-try-tiss sin-eh-ray-ah)
Bourgogne (boor-gon-yuh)
Brouilly (brew-yee)
Brut (brute)
Cabernet Sauvignon (cab-air-nay so-veen-yohn)
Chalonnaise (shah-loh-nez)
Chambertin (shahm-bair-tan)
Chambolle Musigny (shahm-bol moo-see-n'yee

Chassagne Montrachet (shah-san-yuh mon-rah-shay)
Chateauneuf-du-Pape (shah-toe-nuff doo pahp)
Chenas (sheh-nass)
Chenin Blanc (sheh-nan-blahn)
Chiroubles (shee-roob'l)
Cinsault (san-so)
Colombard (cohl-om-bar)
Clos (cloh)
Cos d'Estournel (coh'se dess-toor-nel)
Cote de Beaune (coat duh bone)
Cote de Nuits (coat duh n'wee)
Cote d'Or (coat door)
Cote Rotie (coat roe-tee)
Dolcetto (dohl-chet-oh)
Ducru Beaucaillou (doo-croo bo-cah-yoo)
Espumoso (ess-poo-mow-so)
Figeac, Chateau (fee-jahk)
Fleurie (fluh-ree)

Fume Blanc (foo-may blahn)

Gevrey Chambertin (jev-ray shahm-bair-tan)

Gewurtztraminer (geh-vairtz-tra-mee-ner)

Givry (jee-vree)

Graves (grahv)

Haut (oh)

Hermitage (air-mee-tahj)

Julienas (jool-yeh-ness)

Kabinett (kah-bee-net)

Leoville Las Cases, Chateau (leh-oh-veel lahss cahz)

Loire (l'wahr)

Maconnais (mah-cawn-nay)

Macon Villages (mac-cawn vee-lahj)

Manzanillo (mahn-thah-nee-yah)

Margaux, Chateau (mar-go)

Marsanne (mar-san)

Medoc (meh-doc)

Mercury (mair-coo-ray)

Merlot (mair-low)

Methode Champenoise (meh-toh'd shahm-pen-wahz)

Meursault (muhr-so)

Montrachet (mohn-rah-shay)

Morey Saint Denis (moh-ray san deh-nee)

Moulin-a-Vent (moo-lan-ah-vahn)

Mourvedre (moor-ved'r)

Mousseux (moo-suh)

Muscadet (mus-cah-day)

Nebbiolo (neh-b'yo-lo)

Nuits-Saint-Georges (n'wee san johrj)

Pauillac (paw-yack)

Petrus, Chateau (peh-troos)

Pinot Grigio (pee-no gree-d'jo)

Pinot Noir (pee-no n'wahr)

Pomerol (paw-meh-rahl)

Pommard (po-mar)

Pouilly Fume (poo-yee foo-may)

Pouilly Fuisse (poo-yee fwee-say)

Provence (pro-vahn'ss)

Puligny Montrachet (poo-leen-yee mohn-rah-shay)

Qualitatswein (kval-ee-tates-vine)

Rheingau (rine-gao)

Rheinhessen (rine-hess-en)

Rheinpfalz (rine-fahl'tz)

Riesling (rees-ling)

Rioja (ree-oh-ha)

Romanee-Conti (roh-man-nay cohn-tee)

Roussanne (roo-sahn)

Saint Emilion (sant eh-mee-l'yon)

Saint Estephe (sant ess-teff)

Saint Julien (sant joo-l'yan)

Sangiovese (san-joh-vay-zeh)

Sauvignon Blanc (so-veen-yohn blahn)

Semillon (seh-mee-yohn)

Sommelier (so-mel-yay)

Spatlese (spayt-lay-suh)

Sylvaner (sil-vah-ner)

Syrah (see-rah)

Trockenbeerenauslese (tra-ken-bear-en-ouse-lay-zuh)

Valpolicella (vahl-poh-lee-chell-ah)

Veneto (veh-neh-toe)

Verdicchio (vair-dik-ee-oh)

Vin (van)

Viognier (vee-oh-n-yay)

Vitis Labrusca (vee-tiss la-brew-sca)

Vitis Vinifera (vee-tiss vin-if-er-ah)

Vougeot (voo-joh)

Vosne-Romanee (vone roh-mah-nay)

d'Yquem, Chateau (dee-kem)

Zinfandel (zin-fan-dell)

Words and Terms

This list includes words and terms commonly found on the front and back labels of wine bottles and in other wine related material.

Balance—When fruit, acid, sugar, tannins and alcohol are in harmony, none predominate.

Barrel Fermented—Some white wines are fermented in small oak barrels instead of large tanks, resulting in more body and complex flavors.

Body—The feel of wine in the mouth; thin, medium or full.

Brix—The percentage of sugar in the grape before fermentation and a guide to the alcoholic content of the finished wine.

Bulk Process—Sometimes called "Charmat." A volume method of producing inexpensive sparkling wine.

Clos—French for an enclosed vineyard. Adapted to some California winery names, six at last count.

Corky or **Corked**—A disagreeable smell and taste due to a bad cork.

Cru—Means "growth" in French and refers to specific vineyards of quality. Think of it as meaning "classification."

Cuvee—A special blend of wines.

Enologist—A winemaker.

Enology—The process of making wine from harvest to bottling.

Enophile—A lover of wine.

Estate Bottled—An indication that the wine was produced at the owner's winery from grapes grown on the property.

Fining—The process of clarifying wine during the aging process. Sometimes egg whites are used.

Finish—The flavors that remain in the mouth after swallowing.

Herbaceous—The flavors of herbs sometimes discerned in Cabernet Sauvignon and Sauvignon Blanc.

Hybrid—A variety of grape developed by crossing two or more different species. Commonly done with European and native American varietals to produce French-American hybrids.

Late Harvest—Grapes picked very ripe to overripe, having a high concentration of sugar. Could also be affected by Botrytis Cinerea (the noble rot, see box on page 75), a mold that concentrates flavor and sugar.

Lees—Sediment generated by fermentation. On a label it means the wine (usually Chardonnay) was aged on the lees, or *sur lie,* to pick up flavor characteristics desired by the winemaker.

Legs—Swirl wine in the glass, then watch the rivulets slowly descend. Indicates fullness or lack of.

Malolactic Fermentation—A secondary fermentation in some white and red table wines that converts harsh malic acids to softer lactic acid.

Nose—The way a wine smells—the aroma and bouquet.

pH—The level of a wine's acidity. The lower the number, the higher the acidity. 3.0 to 3.6 is a good range. If lower, the wine may be abrasively tart, higher the wine would taste flat.

Reserve, Private Reserve, Special Reserve, Proprietor's Reserve—Used to indicate wines the producer considers special. The phrases are not regulated and are too often inappropriate or just plain meaningless.

Residual Sugar—The amount of sugar remaining in a wine after fermentation. Often stated on sweet-finished wines as a guide. Slight sweetness becomes apparent to most palates at 0.5% to 1.0%.

Sommelier—French for "wine waiter." In better restaurants. Usually in charge of all wine service from cellar to dining room.

Still Wine—Non-sparkling table wine.

Table Wine—Any white, pink or red wine that is naturally fermented. Usually consumed with food. Must contain at least 7% alcohol and no more than 14%.

Sulfites—Wines containing sulfites (sulphur dioxide) must so state on a label. Sulfites are widely used to preserve freshness in fruits and vegetables and are also a natural byproduct of fermentation. Up to 10 parts per million may be produced by the yeast (well under government standards). A small percentage of people are allergic to sulfites and, of course, should avoid foods that contain them.

Toasty—Used to describe the aromas and flavors imparted from fermenting and aging the wine in oak barrels or casks.

Viniculture—Covers the entire process of growing, making and marketing wine.

Viticulture—Grape growing.

Vinification—The process of turning grape juice into wine.

Vintner—One who sells wine, a wine merchant.

Vintage—On the label, the year in which the grapes were harvested and the wine was born.

References

The following reference books were consulted in preparing this booklet. I list them for those of you wishing to pursue further wine knowledge. They are marvelously well done by some very erudite wine people.

New Frank Schoonmaker
Encyclopedia of Wine—
Revised by Alexis Bespaloff
Pub. William Morrow & Co.

New Connoisseurs' Handbook
Of California Wines
by Norman S. Roby and Charles E. Olken. Pub. Alfred A. Knopf

Parker's Wine Buyer's Guide
Third Edition
Pub. Simon & Schuster

The Simon & Schuster Pocket Guide
To California Wines
by Bob Thompson

Alexis Lichine's New Enyclopedia
Of Wines and Spirits
Pub. Alfred A. Knopf

Hugh Johnson's Pocket Encyclopedia
Of Wine
Pub. Simon & Schuster

Hugh Johnson's The World Atlas
Of Wine
Pub. Simon & Schuster

Making Sense of California Wine
by Matt Kramer
Pub. William Morrow & Co.

In addition to books about wine, one can keep up on doings in the wine world through several wine periodicals. Some of the more popular magazines are: *The Wine Spectator, The Friends of Wine, Wine Trader, Wine Enthusiast,* and *The Wine Advocate.*

Also check the weekly food section of your newspaper. The larger ones carry timely articles on wine, local wine events, best buys in the area, etc. Winemaker dinners provide an excellent means of learning about wine and food.

Finally, don't overlook the opportunities to take a course in wine. Many local universities offer extension courses and there are Continuing Education Centers in some areas that offer wine appreciation courses at very modest fees.

From wine what sudden friendship springs!

JOHN GAY

Index

PHOTO BY BOB MAHON

Dick Patton calls his Chicago years in advertising and merchandising his "first life." Now, with over 35 years in the study of wine, he is enjoying his second life in San Diego—collecting, teaching, judging, writing and consulting.